T0340261

EXTRACTS FROM LETTERS WRITTEN BY
ALFRED B. McCALMONT, 1862-1865

METALMARK BOOKS

Lt.-Col. A. B. McCalmont,
1863.

EXTRACTS FROM LETTERS

WRITTEN BY

ALFRED B. McCALMONT,

Late Lt.-Col. 142d Regt., Col. 208th Regt. and Brev. Brig.-Gen.
Pennsylvania Volunteers.

FROM THE FRONT

DURING

THE WAR OF THE REBELLION.

HORATIO: "I saw him once, he was a goodly king."

HAMLET: "He was a man, take him for all in all,
I shall not look upon his like again."

Printed for private circulation by his son,
Robert McCalmont.

TO THE SURVIVORS

OF THE

PETROLEUM GUARDS

The boys who went out with him, and with whom, but
for an unjust law, he would have come home, this book
is respectfully dedicated.

INTRODUCTORY.

A few years ago the late Col. John S. McCalmont presented to the writer a lot of letters he had received from his brother, Gen. Alfred B. McCalmont, that covered almost the whole period of the latter's life. It was the writer's purpose to publish them entire, but a dozen reasons to the contrary prevented. But as the persons who would most enjoy reading them are rapidly becoming fewer, this reprint of his war letters has been produced. Space considerations required that nothing but war incidents be printed, while many of them are of too personal a nature to allow of their publication. But it is believed that what remains will take the survivor of the 142nd or 208th once more, step by step, through the scenes of his soldierly career, and from time to time unlock the floodgates of his *own* memory as to pleasant occurrences (his mind, probably, needs no such stimulous for the horrible side of war) and thus enable him to relive in thought what he so gallantly lived in deed. Should this end be gained in even a small measure the purpose of this publication will have been amply achieved.

And now a word on two important subjects. It was at first thought that the severe criticisms of President Lincoln should be excised, but second thought made this seem to be taking unwarrantable liberties with historical evidence. Besides, extended inquiry by the writer demonstrated the fact that General McCalmont's opinion of the Commander-in-Chief was not solely his, but was pretty generally the opinion at the time of the whole Army at the front. In later days his opinion of "the man with the cap" was completely changed and no one in the country more sincerely deplored "the deep damnation of his taking off." In the latter days of the war President Lincoln and General McCalmont became acquainted, and the writer has a flask, from the mouth of which during one of his visits to City Point, the President took "a democratic drink in a democratic manner."

Now, as to the change from the 142nd to the 208th. General McCalmont explained to the men of the 142nd when he asked them their opinion, that it would give him promotion—a thing impossible if he remained with his depleted regiment. But he told his wife, the "little woman," who, with a courage and constance as great as his own, cheered and encouraged him through all those "troublous times," that the only consideration that induced him to even think of the change was that by it some, at least, of his subordinates could get their well-deserved promotions.

It is to be regretted, possibly, that the accounts of battles are so meagre. Two obvious causes account for this; letters—long ones at least—are the products of leisure, not activity, while reports of fights would be handed around and often lost to the owner. Still isn't it better on the whole that if any letters were lost it *was* these rather than the graphic descriptions of marches, retreats and pursuits, or the humorous anecdotes and charming descriptions of camp life during inaction.

R. McC.

Franklin, Pa., April 23, 1908.

Fort Massachusetts, near Washington,
Sept. 5, 1862.

My Dear Brother:

We have certainly got along very rapidly. Ten days ago my company was at Franklin, and hardly able to form a straight line, and here they are encamped in tents, and detailed for picket duty as if they were veteran troops. I can hardly realize the rapidity of our organization. You know something of military life and you will know how we must have moved our boots to be here armed and equipped and all encamped in Sibley tents which we got in Washington. I never worked harder than I have worked for the last week. One night at Harrisburg I sat up and copied twelve rolls of my company so as to draw their pay. The next night we were on our way to Baltimore where we arrived at 3 o'clock in the morning. We marched over to the Camden depot in Baltimore in very good order and notwithstanding the lateness of the hour flags and handkerchiefs were waved from many windows to encourage and cheer us. I think that morning and the next were our most dreary. We had had no sleep and the solemn deathlike stillness of a city an hour before daylight has a chilly effect on the nervous system. But there was something bold and confident in the very beating of drums at that hour which argued well for our cause. A year ago the President himself wouldn't have done it.

We were detained at Baltimore until sundown. Other regiments had precedence. The day was beautiful and the men enjoyed their stay very much, but seemed eager to go on. It was after midnight on Wednesday morning when we arrived at Washington. The men got a cup of coffee and some bread and had to lie down on porches and on the bare ground without overcoats. We had met a dozen trains between Baltimore and Washington loaded with the wounded. We had heard news of disaster and defeat and of the probable impending capture of Washington, and yet when daylight came and our boys saw (for the first time to many of them) the National Capitol they exhibited no evidence of apprehension. Early in the morning of Wednesday we were ordered to march to the War Department, but on arriving at the corner of Seventh and Pennsylvania avenue the Colonel (Cummins) joined us and gave me orders to march to this point. He did not come with us. We marched in good order five miles, only resting twice, and again slept on the bare ground, our tents not having arrived in time. Yesterday the tents were put up and now we look like a portion of the army. We are encamped in a beautiful spot just where the Fourteenth street road and the Seventh street road meet.

Well, all the above is very nice, but we have just got orders to march to Halls Hill with 100 rounds of ammunition.—Good-bye. We are marching along. The world still moves.

The Colonel has just had a hearty laugh at my expense. I had fitted up my tent elegantly, and had it all floored and arranged neatly. I was nearly as comfortable as in a parlor.

Fort Massachusetts.
Sept. 9, 1862.

Dear Brother:

Our orders to leave this point were countermanded. We will probably remain here some time.

Major Knox was with me all night. His regiment is a few miles further out the road. He looks well and is a fine soldier.

Tell Whittaker to put a notice in his paper stating that all letters for the Petroleum Guards should be addressed to 142 Regt. Pa. Vol., Washington, and whether we move or not the soldiers will get them in good time. Our men are all detailed to cut down the woods in front of the fort, and to work on the fortifications.

Fort Massachusetts, Sept. 19, 1862.
Friday Morning.

My Dear Brother:

It requires as you know some days to get all little private arrangements made in camp, so as to be able to have your time at your command. The public arrangements are still slower. To get our bread and meat, we had to send our requisitions seven miles to Headquarters, and to get anything else, we had to go through the same motions, besides sending to town for the article, after we had got the order. But we have, at last, got a pretty good supply of wagons, tents, clothing, forage, ammunition and provisions, stationery, blanks, etc., and I can assure you that they had to be carried in detail, at the expense of all our strategy, and that when we captured any one item in the list, at the end of two days' riding and writing we thought we had accomplished something magnificent. Great was the rejoicing in the evening, when the Quartermaster would return, after riding twenty miles circular, and wiping the perspiration from his face, announce that he had gained a point—a victory over red tape—and that, on the following day some article essential to comfort would certainly arrive. Great, too, was the exaltation when our own four wagons with four mules to each were driven into the camp; but greater still the merriment on discovering that the movements of the mules aforesaid were somewhat capricious, and that in all probability it would prove to be easier to carry the provisions than to drive the stubborn brutes. Several men, who had been ambitious to be teamsters, resigned in disgust, and their places were soon supplied by men from the coal fields and furnaces who understood the peculiarities of the animals. So, at last, our equipment was complete. We could say with the witch in Macbeth, "Now I'm furnished. Now I'm furnished." But human beings are never contented. The men are very comfortable and they will probably never, during the service, see such pleasant quarters, and such accommodations as they have here; but still they complain that they came down here to fight and not to do furnace work. For my part I am not particularly eager to hurry into the field. We

will probably have enough of war before we are done.
The old troops are evidently very tired of their life.
They could not have sustained another defeat without be-
coming completely demoralized.

I rode out with Colonel Cummins yesterday to Lees-
boro—about five or six miles—to escort Major Knox,
who was going to rejoin the regiment. Knox has re
gained his health in a good degree, but he is not yet as
strong as he should be to undergo the fatigue of camp
duty, and of daily conflicts. I had a great deal of conversation with Knox. He has a very clear head and gave
me a very entertaining account of the war on the penin-
sula and at Bull Run. Knox is a much better man every
way than I ever suspected. I did not know how much
there was in him.

Coming back the Colonel and I were riding at a run,
when his horse fell with him and threw the Colonel over
his head. The ground was soft and sandy, so that neither
he nor the animal was hurt; but, for a moment I thought
that one or the other was killed. Considering the rate
at which we were going, it was a very lucky escape.

My horse gives me great satisfaction. He is very
gentle, and you can ride him all day without tiring. He
is very much like Ridgway's in appearance and color, but
I would not give him for Ridgway's. I want another
horse of the rough and tough kind, but I presume I can
pick one up some place.

Camp, near Berlin, Md.
Oct. 29, 1862.

My Dear Brother:

I received yours of the 22nd this morning and was
delighted to get news from home of so late a date. I
wrote to my wife yesterday and I presumed that we
would go across the river to-day; but it is by no means
certain. It is now nearly four o'clock in the afternoon.
The Colonel and I were down at Berlin a little while
ago, and troops and wagons were crossing pretty rapidly

on the pontoon bridge. The First Brigade of our Division will, however, probably move before us, and it was not moving as we came past. Berlin presents just now a vivid contrast between the results of war and peace. A fine bridge across the river is in ruins, and beside it the troops and baggage trains are passing on the military structure. Trains of cars are passing on the railroad, carrying passengers on their ordinary business, while artillery wagons are waiting to cross the track. Stopping for a moment on the top of the hill overlooking the river I felt more sadly than I ever did before in relation to this war. But there is no use thinking or talking now. The thing must be fought out, and there is no help for it.

In my letter to my wife I endeavored to give some faint idea of the miseries of Sunday night. Fortunately such nights are not very frequent under similar circumstances. Had we been halted a half an hour sooner we could have made some preparations for the weather and provided good fires at least; but as we did not halt until dark we had poor chances for fuel, and could not select the dryest locations. Col. Cummins selected a spot near a stone fence and part of the night he slept on the top of it. I believe he had the most comfortable berth, but you can imagine from that how the rest were provided. Poor Hiram, the orderly, got a place near the fire, and next to the fence, and nobody had the meanness to disturb him. He seemed to sleep well. I made several ineffectual efforts to get a nap, and finally gave it up. I never passed such a night. Between the constant rain, the cold and smoke it was impossible to get rest. I think a fellow on horseback would have been much more comfortable than I was.

Since Monday morning the weather has been beautiful; but the nights are quite cold. Last night as well as the two previous ones we slept without tents and we have very poor fare, but I think I can stand anything now but being wet. I shall turn my attention to keeping myself dry.

The papers talk of the troops being clamorous for an immediate advance. I presume you are aware that this is all bosh. I don't speak now of the new levies. The old officers and men seem to be very much disappointed by the advance. They had hopes of getting into winter quarters, and were in a very poor condition to move. They were very poorly provided with clothes and wagons.

I will not be allowed under the regulations to carry my trunk. I must provide myself with a valise or carpet bag. So I shall send my (I mean *your*) trunk home, and grin and bear it as well as possible.

Burnside's Corps is already across the river. People at home can talk very learnedly and wisely about onward movements. I should like to see one of these knowing ones undertake to move a single division across a river. One such day as Sunday night utterly defeats the best arranged plan of attack. The roads had been perfectly dry the day before, and yet artillery wagons with six horses to them were in some places unable to move. We are already stinted in forage. What we shall do in Virginia I do not know. I presume my pretty horse will starve. I think a great deal of him. He is a very pleasant animal to ride and very gentle.

I saw General McClellan yesterday. He was riding down an obscure street in the little village. Abe Smith, of the 10th, pointed him out to me. The General was directing or overlooking the crossing of the troops. Maj. Knox and Capt. Over called at our camp this morning. They found me cutting up a hickory tree for firewood.

I am in right good health, but am entirely satisfied that you could not have lived through the war, even if you had escaped bullets. It is a very hard life, and must be a mere succession of annoyances and vexations to a man in delicate health.

I ought to have two horses to carry my blankets and other things; but I presume they would be starved. It is impossible to get any hay for the one I have, and half the time I get no oats..

Near the top of South Mountain and on its Eastern
slope an officer pointed out to me where Maj. Gen. Reno
was killed. The thoughts that I have attempted in the
following verses were suggested then but not expressed
in writing for some months:

A. B. McC.

And here it was, you tell me, that the gallant Reno fell,
Where the morning's beams come soonest, but where evening's
    shadows dwell.
His manhood's dawn was early, his fate has been the same;
So near the mountains summit—so near the height of fame.

Then leave me for a moment, I would linger here alone,
For the scene recalls around me dear memories now my own—
Of the village, of the playground—loves early and sincere,
All tenderly connected with the form that perished here.

How we read and hoped together in the happy days long gone,
Nor dreamed of scenes of war and woe in the dark time com-
    ing on;
As children in yon valley with its Autumn tinge of blue,
Who little care how wild the steep that bounds their distant view.

But the gathered storm has broken—the struggle has begun,
The brother wars with brother, the father with the son
And contrasts sad and striking most fearfully combine
To make the features of the strife that crush hearts like thine.

Yet thou hast perished nobly; for wise men from afar
Will muse among these lovely scenes where ebbed the tide of war,
And will link thy name in story with England's kindred son
Who said 'I die content" when Quebec's bold heights were won.

The brave have closed thy eyelids—the great have borne thy bier,
And proudly paid their homage to the soul that knew no fear;
But other hearts will mourn thee with the summers of the past,
And wear thy image tenderly while life and memory last.

Autumn of 1862.

Camp, near Waterford,
Oct. 31, 1862, Friday.
London Co., Virginia,
Half way between Lovetsville and
Waterford.

My Dear Brother:

The within letter was not mailed at the proper time, and after it was returned to me to-day I doubted the propriety of sending it. But perhaps it may still reach you as soon as other letters written at Berlin.

We halted at this camp yesterday, and remained here making out the muster rolls for pay. It is now evening, and the weather is so mild that a little knot of officers are very pleasantly chatting inside of our tent without fire, and I am able to write comfortably on a small table in the corner. The wagons have overtaken us, and brought our camp equipments. Hereafter, I think, we will take better care of ourselves and not be caught in such a miserable predicament as we were on Sunday evening.

I slept with Major Knox last night. The 10th is encamped just across the road in the woods. That regiment is in the Third Brigade—ours is in the Second. The 121st (Lt. Col. E. W. Davis) is in the First. So we have nearly all Venango companies (but the cavalry) in the same Division, and we find ourselves together at the close of each day's march. Knox is in fine health and spirits. He thinks we will have a fight very soon. His opinion is that the corps on this side of the Blue Ridge will attempt to cross the mountain to flank the enemy and that a battle will be the result, unless the Confederates have concluded to abandon the northern part of the Shenandoah. Knox does not think that we are going to Alexandria. I think that if the enemy retreats toward Richmond without a stubborn battle, McClellan will resume his original plan and embark his troops. But I have written enough. Good night.

Camp, near Warrenton, Virginia,
Nov. 8, 1862, (Saturday).

My Dear Brother:

I received your letter yesterday containing the sad intelligence of Juliet's death. She was a good girl and is doubtless happier now than any of us can be in this world of change and suffering. What a poor farce existence would be if there were no hope of a future.

I wrote to my wife yesterday evening. I have written several letters to her and you and if they have reached their destination you will have a pretty accurate account of our line of march from Berlin on the Potomac to this point. But they may have been lost and therefore it will do no harm to recapitulate.

We left Berlin on Thursday, Oct. 30, and encamped that evening on Kettoctan creek, near Waterford. We stayed at that camp all the next day and left it on Saturday morning, Nov. 1. On Saturday evening we encamped between two lines of half finished railroad. We heard heavy firing in the direction of Snickers Gap all that Saturday and Sunday. We spent Sunday on picket, and on Monday, Nov. 3, about 11 o'clock started toward Snickers Gap. On Monday evening we came to a little village on the main road leading to the Gap. We learned during the day that the firing on the two previous days had been a fight between Pleasanton's cavalry and some mounted artillery on our side and some of the enemy's cavalry and six thousand infantry. I think it must have been a very respectable little affair. It resulted in our forces getting possession of Snickers Gap. It is clear now to my mind that McClellan must have anticipated a much more serious contest at that point, for he was moving a very large force in that direction, and they have since been moved to this point. From the village (Hamilton's store) perhaps? we moved on near sundown on Monday directly toward Snickers Gap, but turned off to the left and encamped on the road toward Union. Our impression was, up to this time, that we were going into the Shenandoah Valley either through Snickers or Ashby's Gap. We marched but a short distance on Tuesday, until the whole Division (Meade's) was halted in a large field, where, after shaking hands with all my friends, I wrote a long letter in pencil to my wife. Then we moved on, in the afternoon, a little farther and encamped near a small stream with a mill dam on it. Some drivers the next morning drowned a mule in it and tried to drown three more. The camp on Tuesday evening was in a beautiful field. We seemed to be surrounded with a pretty large force of our own men, all in very compact shape. Our whole division was in a twenty-acre field, and away around us in other fields in sight and hearing were not less than twenty thousand men. They were all in good spirits, and the evening being pleasant, the drums were beating on every side and a fine brass band was playing at no great distance. I think it was by far the most agreeable night I have spent in the army. We had our tent with us. The wagons are always on hand after a pleasant day's march, when least needed; but never come up on a dreary wet evening when they are indispensable.

The next morning our faces were turned eastward. The advocates of the Alexandria theory of operations began to intimate that they knew more than other people and that they were now certain we were going to the Potomac to embark on transports. When we came on to the main turnpike leading to Alexandria at a town called Middleburg, and started directly east, the Alexandria school of philosophers seemed to be triumphant. But we had not gone far, when we observed the First Brigade turning to the right, and it soon got noised along the ranks that we were going to White Plains that very night. The Blue Ridge was now far behind, and we came into a mountainous country. As we wound up the road from the valley the air felt fresh, keen and sharp, reminding one of the atmosphere in the vicinity of Rattlesnake tavern. After dark it began to rain, and the poor soldiers, wet and shivering, had to march on over a rough road until midnight. Then we poked through the village of White Plains, a melancholy, deserted looking town on the railroad. Nearly all the houses are without any occupants but straggling soldiers. Fortunately it ceased raining before we reached our camping place and having procured some hay and covered myself with gum blankets, I had a comfortable sleep.

The next day's march (Thursday's) brought us to Warrenton, where we now are. The enemy occupied the town until we came in sight and we heard of our cavalry skirmishing with theirs about four miles from Warrenton. But the Rebel force was not very large it seems, and we had no serious engagement. I was not at all disappointed. Our troops marched through the village with colors flying, but without music, and we have since been encamped outside and south of the town.

Yesterday was a rough, cold day. It snowed and the wind blew dismally. The scene around was very dreary. This spot in summer is a fashionable watering place, but it is sad enough now. The stores are closed and the people seem to be feeling the iron heel of war.

Yesterday I met a lawyer whom I knew in Washington. His name is Chilton. He defended John Brown. He helped me to get some things I needed. He says the feeling south is more favorable to compromise than it was. The defeat of the Republicans in the late elections has something to do with it, so he says. Chilton was opposed to our party when I knew him.

Our regiment is ordered out on picket. I must close.

> *Camp, near Rappahannock Station,*
> *Saturday, Nov. 15, 1862.*

My Dear Brother:

We are still at the same point at which we arrived on Tuesday. Orders to be ready to march on short notice were received yesterday, but things don't wear an active appearance. I see no signs of going to-day at least. It is now afternoon.

On Thursday evening the right wing of our regiment went out on picket. The Colonel stayed in camp. I was officer of the picket guard. There were two regiments on the line beside ours. Half of ours is allowed to relieve the whole of one of the old ones. They are reduced to a mere handful.

I rode clear over the picket line about dark and sat up all night. After the moon rose about two o'clock I rode over the line. Again the 10th was on the left, but the old officers are too sharp to be caught doing any unnecessary duty. I found Charley Mackey at one post. He was wide awake. I guess it was too cold to sleep, and he was warming himself by a fire. At one of the posts near him the man on guard had left his post and was sitting by the fire. I didn't make any unnecessary fuss about it.

Yesterday I stopped a quartermaster with eight wagons who was going out to forage. He intended to make a descent on the property of a widow who lived just outside of the line. I told him he must have an order from the General. He sent a sergeant back for the order, but didn't get it. The quartermaster was a cousin of my wife—Sam Evans, of Lancaster.

Yesterday afternoon some of our picket fires set fire to the woods and a large field of dry grass. It made a formidable looking conflagration for a time and would have spread to a great distance if the wind had not changed very suddenly.

That was a singular escape that Steele's Hotel made. I was much entertained with your account of it. The railroad news, too, is interesting.

I should spin this letter out to some extent, if my fingers were warmer. But the air to-day is cold. Major Knox called this morning. He is in good health, but much disgusted with the powers that be. He is one of the officers who see in McClellan's removal nothing but danger. The army does not appear to be moving as fast since McClellan left as it was before.

Some of our men are being tried to-day by a court-martial (division) for marauding. The same men have already been punished by standing on a barrel with a leg of mutton and the word "Thief" on their backs. So you see *Rebel property* is still protected under the new and energetic policy of the administration. I am going over at 2 o'clock to see how the proceedings are conducted and to act as counsel for the men, if it is allowable. I see they are entitled to counsel, but I don't know whether I will be allowed to appear.

Well, I have been at the court-martial. General Jackson was President. Capt. Over is a member. A captain named Porter is Judge Advocate. His father, A. H. Porter, used to keep store in Franklin. I was permitted to appear for the accused. I attempted to make the defense that the men were destitute of food, but it was no use. I presume my client is convicted. Only one man was tried. The court adjourned to meet on Monday.

This is a clear, cold evening. A fire at the door of our tent makes it quite comfortable to write in. I think I shall drop a line to my wife before retiring. The camp looks very cheerful. A thousand fires are burning all around, and drums are beating tattoo.

Give my love to mother for me, and remember me kindly to all friends. I presume you have read the Prince de Joineville on McClellan's campaign. Just now it will produce an immense sensation. It has been now a week since little George was removed. No material advance has been made. In two weeks the army will probably be compelled by bad roads and the cold to go into winter quarters. If something is not done soon the administration will be in a bad way. But they are ruined at any rate. The President is a miserable, weak-minded man— the pliant tool of any person who happens for the time to have his confidence. He was very bold from Springfield to Harrisburg. "Nobody was hurt"—but he mounted a Scotch cap and cloak to come through Baltimore. He talked boldly in his inaugural, but simmered down into the defensive for one whole month. Got brave again and concluded to re-enforce Sumpter and got braver when the people called for vengeance. Bull Run restored the Scotch cap policy and he determined to conciliate the border states. After he got them he concluded they were not essential. He stuck to McClellan till the capitol was safe, but deserted him when he was fighting before Richmond and called on him for help after the second Bull Run. The Scotch cap policy continued to prevail until South Mountain and Antietam had saved the country and until McClellan had driven the enemy far enough to render the capitol safe again. Such miserable shifting and turning would ruin any cause. If the country is not divided it will be because God has determined to preserve it and has chosen the foolish things (Lincoln for instance) to confound the wise. He selected ignorant men to preach His gospel that it might be evident that the works were His own, and it is possible that He intends to demonstrate His power to save our nation in spite of the rebels in arms and fools in council.

Camp, near Stafford Court House.
Thursday, Nov. 20, 1862.

My Dear Brother:

I believe my last letter to you was written at our camp, near Rappahannock station on Saturday or Sunday last. I have since written to my wife, but as she is at Pittsburg you will not probably see the letter. So I will resume my chronicle of the glorious 142nd where I left it on Sunday.

On Sunday afternoon Major Knox, Colonel Cummins and myself took a ride out around our camp as far as the picket lines. We visited a signal station where some officers were trying to send messages to a point on the mountain ten miles distant, but could not do it for the smoke from the camps. The signal officers told me that with a clear atmosphere they can send a message forty miles without repeating. It seems almost incredible.

Our conversation during the ride was chiefly on the probable change in the direction of the army. We had seen a large body of our troops, Cox's Corps, passing the camp on the road toward Fredericksburg. They had come from a point west of Warrenton and had been fired upon on Saturday by a rebel battery from the opposite side of the river. This, together with the fact that it has been arranged to burn the bridge across the river at the station, were regarded as indications of a change of program. On Sunday evening we received orders to be ready to march on Monday morning at 7 o'clock. The movement commenced very promptly and after we had passed the railroad and heard that the bridge had been burned, all doubt about our destination passed away. I freely admit that when I was perfectly assured that the march lay toward Fredericksburg, I felt a sense of relief. The prospect of success at this season with any other General than McClellan, on the ground where Pope's reverses began, was very dim. The old officers regarded a march toward Gordonsville under a new commander as a very dangerous experiment.

We made twenty miles on Monday's march. The morning was rather cold, with a drizzling rain. Our rests were very short, and we did not halt until after dark. Then we had to encamp in the woods. The Colonel and I made a nice tent with our gum blankets and slept well after a pretty good supper. On Tuesday morning we started on in the same direction, but about 11 o'clock, while resting in an open field, our whole brigade got orders to march in echelon. We usually wait until all the other regiments get in motion, and take up their line of march along the road. This gives us a longer rest. But the change of order took us by surprise. My horse had to be bridled and, of course, I was not ready. But nobody said anything. We soon joined in the movement. Then we were marched by the right flank (the whole division) into another big field across the road where all the troops were halted, each regiment being in line of battle. General Reynolds' staff rode past us two or three times. There were some of our troops ahead of us on a hill. They seemed to be sending out skirmishers, and we heard some little firing in the woods. I have not learned that it was either known or believed that the enemy was about, at that time, but for a few minutes things looked a little strange. I think there was nothing in the movement but what was necessary to change the direction of the corps toward this point. At any rate, we left the Fredericksburg road there, and came on over a rough country covered with little pines to a small creek, where we are now halted. I have seen a map of eastern Virginia to-day, and I have made a rough sketch from memory, to show you where we are. We came here on Tuesday evening, and it has been raining nearly ever since. The longer it continues the worse it gets. Our men have been out to-day making corduroy roads. Captain Hasson was out with a party. He returned this evening wet and tired. He had gone out to a point near Stafford Court House. He says the roads are terrible, and that some wagons he saw could hardly get along. He heard that our troops had possession of Falmouth and the rebels possession of Fredericksburg. It would seem that the intention now is to mass our troops between Aquia creek and Fredericksburg on the line of the railroad. Whether the plan is to go into winter quarters here or embark on transports for James river we don't know. Various speculations are afloat about it. If it is intended to go into winter quarters, the movement would, to my mind, seem to have been premature. It looks more like embarking. One thing is certain, we cannot march to Richmond by way of Fredericksburg with bad roads at this season.

I walked over to General Meade's headquarters at 2 o'clock to attend the court-martial of our marauders. I believe I told you about the proceeding. Six of our men walked out from camp and saw another soldier (one of the old troops) with a calf which he had killed. He proposed that if they would help skin it they should have a share. They assented, but after the division of the spoil they were arrested. The old soldier escaped. Our men were punished on sight by General Reynolds by being placed on a barrel with the word "Thief" and the veal on their backs for an hour, and now they are being tried by court-martial. All this is under the new administration. I appeared to-day for the offenders and made a short speech. One advantage of doing this will be to learn something of proceedings in military courts.

Well, having told you this before, I presume it will be very uninteresting. I was going to tell you that in the morning a person could walk to General Meade's headquarters without difficulty, but when I returned this evening the camp was one vast mire. It is now late in the evening and the rain is pouring down steadily. I consider the fall campaign in this region closed. This day settles the question.

I am in good health and spirits. Half of our regiment, the left wing, with the Major is out on picket. They have a rough night for it. I took the last turn with the right wing at the old camp.

Camp, near Aquia Creek,
Saturday, Nov. 22, 1862.
My Dear Brother:

I have already told you that while we lay at the camp near Stafford Court House it rained almost incessantly. During two or three days large fatigue parties were out making corduroy road. The object appeared to be to get supplies from Aquia creek. Last evening early we got an order to detail one hundred men from our regiment for fatigue duty. The other regiments were required to furnish each a proportionate number. The men and company officers grumbled considerably at the order, because many of the soldiers were nearly bare-foot, and none of them had even a full supply of hard crackers. This state of things, a result of the "masterly evacuation of Warrenton," was bound to become worse, unless we either made a road to the new base of supplies, or else marched there. It seemed to be the intention at sundown yesterday to make the road, but before bed-time a different conclusion was arrived at by the General, and we got orders after retiring countermanding the detail for fatigue duty and requiring us to be ready to march at 7 this morning "punctually." Accordingly at the appointed hour, the division was in motion. I stayed behind our regiment to see that everything belonging to the Colonel and myself was put in our wagons. The camp ground looked very desolate after the men had gone. Our tent had been pitched near a deserted house under a weeping willow. Immediately in front of it was a small private burying ground, where some crude head stones and a

few locust trees marked the resting place of some of the
old generation.   A few old posts were left of what had
once been a substantial fence.   These were used for fuel
by the soldiers.   The locust trees fared the same fate;
and when I turned to look at the spot this morning, there
was nothing left but the willow tree and the grave stones,
from which time had effaced their rude inscriptions.
Down below, on the creek, near the camp, appeared to
be the ruin of some old manufactory.   Yesterday the
sound of drums, the bright fires of the camp, the jeering
and laughing of a few thousand men had, in spite of dismal weather and gloomy, pine-covered hills, given some
animation to this dreary and desolate spot, but to-night
there is nothing there but the ruins of man's labor, and
the sad memorials of his mortality.

The march to-day was attended with no incident worth
mentioning.   It lay through a miserable looking country, covered with dwarf pine trees and here and there
marked by the ruins of some old plantation, from which
fences and houses have disappeared, but where old and
dying fruit trees gave evidence that men had once lived
and labored and died or gone away.   The soldiers
marched through the woods, following a blazed track
not far from a poor country road.   Sometimes I had to
dismount and lead by horse, but generally I could make
my way on horseback with some little rubbing and
scratching.   We occasionally crossed the road, over which
by the aid of corduroy improvements, the ambulances,
buggies, wagons and artillery were making slow and
tedious progress.   We could hear the drivers whipping
and swearing, and sometimes see a wagon stuck fast in
the mud.   On the way a boy met us with the "Philadelphia Inquirer," and there was a great deal of laughing
over one of the headings of army news which pithily
stated in substance, but in large capitals, that the army's
advance was not impeded by the rain.   Before noon we
reached Stafford Court House.   That is literally the
thing and nothing else.   I saw but three buildings.   There
may have been four—some one said so.   One man con-
veyed his opinion of the country by saying, "If this d—d
hole is the Court House, I wonder what the devil the jail

is like." We did not stop at the county seat, but came on without much rest to this place—a point on the Richmond, Fredericksburg & Potomac R. R.—four miles from Aquia Creek station, which is the river terminus of the road. Here we are encamped on a hill commanding a view of the railroad and a considerable portion of the surrounding country. We have already commenced to receive crackers, for the want of which the men were absolutely suffering. We have got our tent up. Several wagons got through about 4 o'clock. They came about five miles in nine hours. This is "onward to Richmond" with a vengeance. Some of them are stuck in the mud.

I shall not advance any opinion about our future movements. You can judge for yourself whether we are going to Richmond by way of Fredericksburg this season. I see by the paper that one wing of the army rests on the Rappahannock, the other on the Potomac. This place was winter quarters for some of the rebels last year. I presume we will be here some days. You had better come and see us.

After coming here to-day I went out and bought a pair of chickens and some potatoes. We are very comfortable, and as steamboats are running twice a day from Aquia Creek to Washington we expect to be comfortable while we remain here. The army seems to be rebuilding bridges on the railroad and putting it in running order. To complete the repairs to Fredericksburg will require two weeks.

Camp at Brook's Station, Virginia,
Friday, Nov. 28, 1862.

My Dear Brother:

I believe I wrote to you from this place two or three days ago, before going out the last time on picket. My letters, however, don't seem to go through regularly. I have a vague notion that the powers that be have no great anxiety for the rapid transmission of intelligence from the soldiers to their friends at home. But I presume all my letters will be forwarded ultimately and perhaps they will be considered by indulgent friends worth a perusal, even though they contain nothing but what has appeared in the papers previously.

I had rather a pleasant time of it on my last turn for picket duty. Our regiment was on the center of the line, the 10th on the left and the 1st, Biddle Robert's old regiment, on the right—just in the order of the three brigades forming Meade's division. I was officer of the picket, and had my headquarters at the house of a man named Schooler on the road leading to Aquia Creek. He has a son in the Rebel army, and I presume is a secessionist, but he gave the officers corn bread and bacon and horse feed, and a good room and a fire, for a pecuniary consideration. As it commenced raining about 9 o'clock at night and continued without interruption till morning, we were of course thankful for even these poor accommodations. Besides, the young ladies at the house were very chatty and they entertained us during the evening. One of them is very pretty. Almost any kind of woman looks lovely to a man who hasn't seen one for some weeks.

Schooler's house is on a high piece of ground commanding a view of the Potomac. I had not seen the river since we left Berlin four weeks ago—and after locating the pickets I rode up to Schooler's house about sundown on Tuesday evening. I was so delighted with the sight of the river and the vessels and steamboats that I paid no attention to the old man's invitation to come in, but sat on my horse a long time enjoying the beautiful view, and thinking about the good old times of peace and union when I had passed along that same old river before.

Knox was on the left. He came over to Schooler's on Wednesday morning, and with Major Tully, of the 1st, we took advantage of our position to ride down to Aquia Creek. But we got very little for our ride. Then we rode back and had a dinner of bacon and krout, and at 3 o'clock were relieved. My superstition about moving the day after being on picket didn't hold good. It is like all similar notions, founded on a false system of generalization, and wasn't reliable. At any rate we are still here, and I predict we will not be twenty miles from this point all winter unless we embark on transports. But no matter about that. Everybody likes to make predictions nowadays, to show his sagacity, but everybody sometimes makes mistakes.

I have just been interrupted. Henry McCalmont—a son of John B., who was a son of Uncle Henry, called and inquired for Hiram. Hiram McCalmont (Henry McCalmont's son), as I told you, is a grandson of Uncle Henry also. I thought Hiram too weak and young for hard service, and the Colonel made him orderly. He is very useful. On the march he rides the Colonel's white horse. By the way, I have been acting Arnold Plumer with my relations in Company I. Prather, a cousin of ours, is sick at Washington. I have written to the Secretary of War to procure his discharge. I had previously made him orderly sergeant. The other night, very late, an order came from headquarters to detail two teamsters on short notice. Hugh Shaw, another cousin, was one of the lucky men. Derby (John Phœnix, Jr.), in his amusing book, hits off in happy style this kind of nepotism. Well, Henry McCalmont (John B's son) belongs to Knox's company of the 83d. He is a fine looking fellow—very unassuming. He has been hit by buckshot twice, but he won't say he was wounded. A Brigadier General would have had such a catastrophe telegraphed about as follows: "General C. —— shot in the face and breast. Surgeon has hopes of his recovery." This morning I had our regiment out by the Colonel's leave on battalion drill. We have it now regularly every morning. I am learning the confounded thing, but by diligent application I might have mastered it all a month ago. The trouble was we never had any drills, and I have not had an opportunity to book much. I succeeded very well this morning—forming divisions—marching to the rear into column—deploying column—changing direction in column closed in mass and "all that sort of thing," as Colonel Magilton would say. I had two questions raised by the Major and Captain Warren, of Mercer, but I was right both times, as they have since admitted. If I had a regi-

ment of my own I should take great pride in drilling it,
and great satisfaction in having its administrative business properly attended to. Colonel Cummins has excellent common sense and judgment, but he always takes
the easiest way of doing everything and won't drill the
regiment unless he is required to. He says it's hard on
the men to turn out without shoes. He has a very kind
heart.

Camp near Brook's Station, Virginia,
Wednesday, Dec. 3, 1862.

My Dear Brother:

I spent part of this day in trying to find out how to get
an order to send Colonel Cummins to a general hospital,
and in preparing the papers after I had learned the way.
The Colonel became sick on Friday evening. He was
at his worst on Monday afternoon, when he consented
that I should telegraph to his wife. He is now better
and out of all danger, but if he had been dying it would
have been all the same so far as his removal was concerned. He would have had to remain in a cold tent
without any of the conveniences which a sick man ought
to have, and breathe his last there without his wife or
friends near him. He first applied for a leave of absence; or rather our Major, who knows a great deal, because he was in the three months' service, undertook to
make the application for him. Well, the application went
on from the regimental headquarters to brigade headquarters and from brigade headquarters to division headquarters and so on, stopping the usual length of time at each,
until it came to somebody who decided that the surgeon's
certificate wasn't strong enough. He should have stated
that further confinement in camp would prove fatal or
produce permanent disability, or words to that effect. So,
of course, the application came back. Yesterday evening
I concluded to see if something couldn't be done by personal application, and I was encouraged by the Medical
Director to change the form of the application, and ask

to have the Colonel removed to a general hospital. So I started this morning, and like Lord Lovell, I rode and I rode, and after writing the application over three times in consequence of confounding two men named Green— one the Brigade Surgeon, and the other Adjutant on General Franklin's staff, I at last got it up to the Medical Director, who assured me that it would be acted on to-morrow and that it would doubtless succeed. This result was particularly satisfactory, inasmuch as when I returned to our quarters I found the Colonel sitting by a fire in Captain Hasson's tent and in such improved health that if the order should come it will be a convenient means of getting our winter supplies from Washington by enabling him to go there; and if it does not come no person will be hurt.

After finishing this piece of business I got out a four-horse wagon and rode out myself on horseback to guide the teamster to Schooler's on the picket line, who, as I had noticed when at his house, had a large quantity of old iron saved from the ruins of the buildings burned last summer at Aquia Creek. I purchased from him, and brought back a large stove in fragments and some bars of iron, a gridiron and an iron bedstead. Then I got Hiram and Bowers to dig a neat ditch for a flue, and covered it with the stove plates and earth. Then we made a chimney, and the thing, on experiment, proved to be a complete success and one of the best contrivances of the kind in the division. Then we were preparing to move our tent so as to have the flue running entirely through and under it, when Colonel Magilton's orderly handed me a small slip of paper. It was only an order for the troops of this brigade to be ready to march to-morrow morning at daylight. This spoiled, for a time, all my plans, and I got some jokes on my labor. Then we all commenced to prepare for the move. Other orders came to have six days' rations, and for distribution of clothing, etc., etc., and finally about 8 o'clock we got an order countermanding the first one. So we do not go to-morrow, but I presume we will go soon. We think the march will not be a long one, unless the troops should be convoyed to the James river by transports. I am too cold to bore you with my ideas of our destination, and they would not be of much value. I am writing by a pine log fire in front of our tent. The night is calm and growing very cold. I must quit and retire.

Camp near Belle Plains, Virginia,
Jan. 13, 1863.

My Dear Brother:

The mail yesterday brought me two letters, one from you and one from my wife, both dated the sixth. They were very interesting. I feel somewhat disappointed now unless I hear from home every day or two.

I have not much to write about. All is dull and unchanged here. We have no orders now to be ready to move. Our court-martial still keeps in session every day trying a lot of trivial charges. We sit in a small dark cabin, very poorly heated, and without a floor. To-day we had four cases to try, all growing out of the whisky ration issued on the 17th of December. I am in hopes that we shall be able to get through, however, in another week.

Our first case was that of Lieut. Col. Peter Baldy, of the 12th, who after the second Bull Run left his regiment and remained absent without leave, more than two months. He was found guilty and sentenced to be dismissed. Colonel Sickles, of the 4th, commanding the division, assumed the responsibility of disapproving the sentence, and ordered Baldy to resume his sword. It was a pretty big stretch of authority for an acting division commander. I suppose, however, it was all right, though the facts would not warrant it, but yesterday an order from corps headquarters pronounced Colonel Sickles' disapproval illegal and directed Lieut. Col. Baldy to remain in arrest until his case can be determined or reviewed by higher authority. Baldy's case was the first one we tried, and it was the only one of any importance that came before us.

I have to stay at the court every day until 2 or 3 o'clock. Then after dinner I attend to the business of the regiment, signing requisitions, etc., and on clear days we have a dress parade. By the time I have finished it is dark, and then occasionally some old friend steps in to spend an hour. Colonel Cummins does not board nor lodge at brigade headquarters. He has not changed his mode of life, and does not put on airs in consequence of being an acting Brigadier.

But though our life is monotonous time goes very fast. I am surprised to think that this month is so nearly half gone. Winter will soon be over, and then the operations of spring will commence. We have not yet received any pay, and I presume we will have to wait until Congress passes a bill to authorize the issue of more money.

You are right about the Abbott note. I am much more anxious now to have a reputation for honesty than for being a soldier. It will be probably much harder to establish. If I should never return, I hope that my debts will all be paid out of my share of father's estate. It ought to be sufficient to cover them, and give my wife and children a home, and leave her property unembarrassed. I mention this now because there is no immediate apprehension of a battle. This kind of talk on the eve of a fight might make you feel as if I had some gloomy forebodings, which is not the case.

Oliver wants the table to get supper.

Camp near Belle Plains, Virginia,
Jan. 17, 1863.

My Dear Wife:

I received your letter of the 9th to-day. I was somewhat surprised to hear that you do not receive my letters regularly. I write nearly every day to you or John. Occasionally I have allowed two days to pass without writing, but this is very rare. Your letters reach me very regularly now. They are six or seven days coming, but they arrive safely, I believe. It is possible that the War Department may for sufficient reasons detain the army mail a few days so as to prevent an early publication of our position or intended movements. I think this has been done more than once since I commenced soldiering. Perhaps it is good policy, though somewhat annoying to friends at home.

At last the Reserves have gotten an answer from the Secretary of War favorable to their application, as made by the Governor, and they are to go back to Washington or Pennsylvania as soon as their place can be filled. I presume they will leave before a week, but it seems our regiment is not going with them. I don't know who our new associates will be, and I do not care much. As I said before, I have made up my mind not to care much about anything. The 121st will probably be with us, and its officers are a pretty good set of men, some of them very intelligent.

James Elliott, of Company I (my old company), is alive. He was taken prisoner and sent to Richmond. I am glad he is safe. I told you in a former letter that he was reported killed, but that I had some doubts about it. I never wrote to the family because I could not write anything but what would have been discouraging. My reasons for believing that Jim was alive were founded on a feature in his character strongly akin to an excess of prudence.

It seems there is some kind of an order for marching at division headquarters. We understand that we are to move in some direction on Monday, but we have not gotten the order yet.

I am still sitting every day on a court-martial. I am President of the Court. I am also acting as commander of the regiment. Colonel Cummins is commanding the Second Brigade. I mention this because you do not seem to understand it. I am not promoted. John can explain it to you. General Meade, you know, was assigned to a new command. Colonel Magilton, who commanded the Second Brigade, resigned about the same time. Colonel Sickle, then being the oldest Colonel in the division, was assigned to the command of the division. Colonel Cummins was then the only Colonel in the Second Brigade. All this was the result of the peculiar features of the act organizing the Pennsylvania Reserves. If you will read the Governor's special mes-

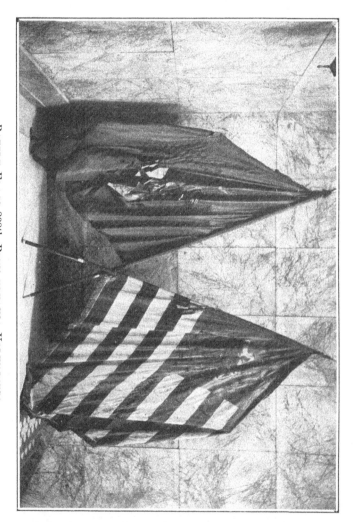

BATTLE FLAGS 208th PENNSYLVANIA VOLUNTEERS,

From a photo taken by the permission of Adjt.-Gen. Thomas Stewart.

sage you will see that a great many regiments in the division are commanded by captains, for instance, the First Regiment (Colonel Biddle Roberts') is now commanded by a Captain (Tally). The Eighth, Dr. Hays' regiment, is commanded by a Major, the Colonel (Dr. George S. Hays) and Lieut. Col. John Duncan, having resigned. There have been no promotions among the officers of the Reserves, because the officers had to be elected. The Governor would not commission them without an election, and the division commanders would not allow an election to be held. This is not the case with any other troops. Read the Governor's special message and you will understand. As our regiment does not belong to the Reserves and was not organized under the same Act of Assembly, our case is different, and our promotions are regular. Colonel Cummins will, I presume, cease to act as Brigadier in a few days, and then I will cease to have command. Now you know all about it. I have used entirely too many words.

The weather is quite cold again. It is very changeable. I was threatened with a sore throat yesterday, but the symptoms have all gone. I am now in excellent health and in good spirits.

Major Knox, of Clarion, left without giving us any notice of his going. He was in our tent the evening before he left, but he did not get his leave of absence until that night.

I saw Lieut. Col. Rogers, of Franklin, yesterday. He and Captain Kennedy called, both looking very well. Rogers is getting fat.

My brown horse has recovered from his wound so far that I can ride him again. I rode him to-day a mile or two. He is a very pleasant animal for my use, and I think a great deal of him.

Tell Colonel Kerr that the horse which he gave me is doing well and is very useful. I feel under great obligations to him.

We have not gotten a cent of pay yet. Hurrah for Mr. Chase, the great financier. Grin and bear a little longer.

Your husband,

A. B. McCalmont.

3

Camp near Belle Plains, Virginia,
Feb. 1, 1863.

My Dear Wife:

The Paymaster arrived yesterday and settled with our regiment for the months of September and October. I received $334. So you perceive my yearly allowance is about $2,000, something less than we formerly lived on, but I presume we can stand it. I cannot safely send you any large amount by mail, but lest you may be in great need, I shall risk enclosing $22 in this letter and continue to make small remittances as often as I write.

Major Louis E. Johnson paid us a visit. He is a son of Reverdy Johnson, the Maryland United States Senator, and formerly Attorney General. The Major, who is our Paymaster, is a fine looking fellow, a little on the Biddle Roberts style, is quite polished and at the same time very willing to take things as they come and make the best of them. He had two clerks with him, both very agreeable fellows. I would have supposed they were city editors or reporters from their interest in everything and their turn for observation. The party spent two nights in our cabin and this morning the sutler furnished a wagon and Hiram went as guide to conduct the gentlemen to the camp of the Third Indiana Cavalry. Hiram says they had a rough time of it. Major Johnson rode my spotted horse. The wagon stuck fast in the mud. They sent back to an artillery battery for horses to draw it out. Then with the aid of four horses they succeeded in reaching the cavalry camp before sundown. The whole distance traveled was about three miles.

While the party remained here we had a very pleasant time of it. We gave them short cake and such other similar luxuries as our circumstances would afford, and they were polite enough to appear to be very much pleased.

There is a great difference in paymasters. Gideon I. Ball, of Erie, is one. He is paying a regiment up in the First Brigade. They say he has been two days in paying one company, and that where a soldier's pay has odd cents in it less than five, Gideon pockets the small amount himself. Johnson is above this small business. To illustrate the difference, if a soldier's pay amounted to $16.83, Ball would give him $16.80, and Johnson $16.85. Our whole regiment appears to be much pleased with Major Johnson. He does not make any unnecessary objections to the rolls, and does the business with great promptness.

I went up to Division Headquarters this afternoon and spent an hour with Lieutenant Colonel Henderson and Colonel Sickle, who commands the Division in General Doubleday's absence. They were not able to give me any fresh information about the proposed withdrawal of the Pennsylvania Reserves to Washington, nor could they tell whether our regiment is to go along. We have heard various rumors about it, as for instance one that General Hooker was opposed to the Reserves going. But I think from General Doubleday's dispatch that they will certainly leave. Whether we go too is uncertain.

The roads are still miserable. It is now raining. The snow is nearly all gone. To-day we sent down horses to the landing and carried up corn and oats in bags. The poor horses had not eaten anything for twenty-four hours.

You need not apprehend a battle very soon even if General Hooker is a great fighter.

I am in excellent health, but this is an awfully dull locality. The only amusement we have is to see the mule teams sticking in the mud and getting pulled out. Love to all.

Camp near Belle Plains, Virginia,
Feb. 4, 1863.

My Dear Brother:

I am no longer on duty in the court-martial. A new one has been organized.

We have received pay for two months up to October 31, 1862. Out of the $334 thus paid I have to clear up my debts here. The rest I will send to you and my wife. I have sent her in one letter $22, and in another $10. I do not like to risk sending a large amount by mail. The mails here are like everything else, they go my military routine. We are only a mile and a half from the steamboat landing; but our letters go first to Brigade Headquarters, then to Division Headquarters, one mile due west; then to Corps Headquarters, three miles further west; then to Grand Division Headquarters, a little further toward the Rappahannock, and finally to the Headquarters of the Army of the Potomac, stopping, I believe, at each Headquarters about twelve or twenty-four hours. After going through this interesting preliminary transition they are sent down to Falmouth and thence by rail over to the Potomac river from which they started. The system is admirable. One cannot help admiring its order, its regularity and precision; but like all other workings of the same system, it is impossible for a plain man to see how the great and desirable result of getting a letter to its destination is hastened by the process. There is a great deal more of method for the sake of method in the army, than of method for the sake of substance.

This morning is very cold. Last night even with a big fire in our cabin we could hardly make ourselves comfortable. I presume we shall have several severe nights now.

There is no news this morning about the Reserves going to Washington; but I believe they will go soon. They are organizing a Division to take their place. This was the last intelligence from General Doubleday, who is at Washington. Colonel Sickle, of the Fourth, is still temporarily in command of this Division, Colonel Cummins temporarily in command of the Second Brigade, and I am temporarily in command of this regiment.

The changes in the army and the recent operations have produced a very marked dissatisfaction. There is but one opinion in regard to the Administration, and it is very freely expressed. The directing power, wherever it may be, is ridiculously incompetent.

But it is too cold to write much.

Harrisburg, May 8, 1863.

Hon. John S. McCalmont:

Your brother Alfred telegraphs me that neither himself nor any of the Venango boys are injured.

E. C. Wilson.

Camp below Falmouth,
May 8, 1863.

My Dear Brother:

I wrote a long letter to my wife to-day giving her a minute account of myself during the past week. I have just learned from Lieutenant Gray that she has gone to Butler, and you will not therefore see the letter immediately, so I shall give you a line or two for your own information.

You know by the papers that our army is all back on the north side of the Rappahannock. I say all, but it is sad to reflect that nearly 2,000 of them are lying in the pine woods, many of them to rot without a burial. I wish some of our war spouting libellers of the Gospel of Peace could see the battlefield.

You know, too, by the dispatches I sent, if they went through, that our Venango boys in Biddle's regiment and ours are safe. Thank God we have been spared by a singular combination of chances that promised just the reverse. They seemed determined to put us in first, and yet it so happened that the First Corps did not sustain any serious loss. I will tell you all about it.

You know, when I wrote last a week ago, our corps was operating at a pontoon bridge below Fredericksburg, just opposite where Meade's division fought on the 13th of December, and about a mile or less from where I now write. Robinson's division and Doubleday's remained on this side of the river. Wadsworth's, the First Division, had crossed, had planted a battery, and dug some rifle pits. General Hooker had informed the army by a general order that the enemy was in a position where he must come out from behind his entrenchments and be defeated, or else ingloriously retreat. But on Friday an order came just as I was closing my former letter that we should cross at 3 o'clock and storm the heights. Three o'clock came, then 4, then 5, and still no movement. The order had evidently been countermanded. I have not learned yet what was wrong, but I was not sorry. The men had no heart for the work. It was simply to advance a mile over a level plain raked by the enemy's guns, and take the rifle pits in the woods. I believe we should have failed, but the next day his force at that point was diminished.

On Friday night we slept in the ravine near the pontoon bridge. Early Saturday morning, May 2nd, we received orders to march. We soon understood that we were to go up the river to join Hooker. It was a bright, beautiful morning and our division had just gotten under arms and were about moving out of the ravine, when the enemy's batteries across the river opened on us. Their shot and shell were all directed toward us. One shell passed close over my head; I was on my horse, and struck the Colonel's horse on the head, tearing off the poor animal's lower jaw and part of the upper. He fell and got up and looked about him. It was a pitiable sight. Then, as the regiment marched off, he followed it. In a short time afterward a battery man killed him to put him out of pain. (Remainder of letter lost.)

*Camp near Falmouth,
Monday, May 11, 1863.*

My Dear Brother:

I have nothing new to write. We are lying in the woods five miles below Falmouth and about a mile from the Rappahannock, just where we were when I wrote last. There are some indications of preparation for a move; but I expect that we will remain here several days.

I think there will be foreign interference before a month, based on the repulses at Charlestown, Vicksburg, and the Rappahannock.

If this army could not hold its position on the other side of the river a week ago, it certainly cannot advance now. We are losing troops daily by the expiration of their time. All the nine-month men (ten regiments), and all the New York two-year men are about leaving. The army is also much dispirited.

> *Camp near White Oak Church, Virginia,*
> *May 20, 1863.*

My Dear Brother:

I have received two letters from you recently. The last was dated May 13, and contained the news of the great oil fire and the burning of the bridge at Franklin. The other letter was about business.

Coop. Cochran paid us a visit on Sunday. It was a beautiful day. We went down into the fields near the Rappahannock, and with the aid of an opera glass viewed the scene of the old battle. Coop. had no difficulty in recognizing the precise spot where the Tenth went in, and where General Jackson was killed. Cattle were quietly grazing on the broad and beautiful ground. Little birds were singing around us. Pickets on each side of the river were lazily lounging on their posts, and seemed to manifest a mutual contempt for the sublime art of war. I doubt whether you could find a more striking contrast than the plains below Fredericksburg have presented very often within the last few months. But you know how lovely they are in the spring.

On Monday morning Coop. left us. Colonel Cummins and I went with him up to the Falmouth station. There we got some articles for our mess. On returning we found our tents all down and the regiment ready to move. We soon learned that there was to be a change of camp, and that some learned doctor was at the bottom of the movement. He had read in some book that large bodies of men have better health when encamped in open fields than when lying in the woods. Accordingly we are now enjoying all the sanitary advantages of a spot destitute of vegetation, poorly supplied with water, and where every breeze comes tainted with the perfumes of defunct horses.

In spite of all these disadvantages the men have by great industry in two days made the prettiest camp we have ever enjoyed. They carried pine trees nearly a mile, and now the streets are all in beautiful order.

Our paroled prisoners and sick men have been returning in great numbers. Among those who have come back to this regiment during the past week was James Elliott, of Franklin, who was taken prisoner December 13. He is in very good health.

On Monday afternoon I rode over to the camp of the Fourth Pennsylvania Cavalry at Potomac Creek railroad bridge. I remained there till yesterday evening. Colonel Kerr and Lieut. Col. R—— were leaving. They have both resigned, Kerr on account of permanent ill health. He appears to be quite weak. He cannot ride a horse faster than a walk without suffering pain. Kerr was very kind to me. He gave me a good military coat, a pair of good gauntlets and a sabre, for all of which he had no further use. Colonel R—— had some difficulty with his regimental line officers. He was not well liked. He requested me to ask Whittaker to say that he had a good reputation as an officer. His resignation was accepted on the ground of his incompetency. But he is *honorably discharged,* and if Whit. is willing to state the latter fact without alluding to the former, it will be fully as much as R—— has any right to expect. So many Venango men have left the service that I presume the rest of us will have to see the thing through.

It is hard to see where the war is going to end. I look for foreign interference very soon, based on the Charlestown and Fredericksburg repulses. England and France have been waiting for a good opportunity to act; and when they do act they will be in earnest. In relation to this meddling with our affairs by the powers of Europe, I feel very much as I did when fighting with Ben McCullough at Washington. Some fellow ran for the police. I did not holler for the police myself, of course, but I thought they were a plagued long time coming.

This army is much reduced. The loss in killed, wounded, and prisoners in the last fight is not far from twenty thousand. The loss by New York two-year men and Pennsylvania and New Jersey nine-month men leaving will not be less than 30,000 more. A regiment goes every day, and some days more. Negro brigades cannot be organized fast enough to supply this drain. So you see the prospect of another immediate advance across the Rappahannock is not very imminent. Indeed we will do well, under present circumstances, to hold our own. But I have written all the news I had. You can make reflections for yourself.

Camp near White Oak Church, Virginia,
May 22, 1863.

My Dear Brother:

I am in my usual good health, with the exception of some bilious symptoms, which a little attention to diet will remove. The army is lying very quietly in the sun. It is too warm to do anything.

Colonel Cummins, would, I think, like to give up his present position if he could get some appointment that would justify him in resigning. He is a strong Republican as you know. Of course, his resignation would inure to my benefit. If you should be in Harrisburg soon or holding any correspondence with Curtin you might mention this thing. Cummins is a pretty good politician. You know he was elected Sheriff of Somerset county.

I have nothing new to write. You might visit the army now, and perhaps get leave to bring some one with you. But the camps are mostly disagreeable from the presence of dead horses. It seems impossible to burn them up fast enough.

P. S.—Private.

There has been a misunderstanding between Reynolds and Hooker. Reynolds is a thorough soldier and somewhat disgusted with humbug. I am told that either Reynolds or Hooker will be relieved, or else our corps will be assigned to duty elsewhere.

Our First and Second Brigades, constituting Doubleday's division, will be soon consolidated. Then some new troops will be added, possibly the Pennsylvania Reserves. There might be such a thing as taking us up to join the Reserves at Washington. There is some change brewing.

Centreville, Virginia,
June 16, (Tuesday).

My Dear Brother:

I presume you know by the papers that the army has come back or is coming to the neighborhood of Washington.

Our corps left camp near White Oak Church on Friday morning. The Sixth Corps remained a day longer, and the pontoon bridge was still kept in its position. But I learn from an eye witness that that corps burned the depot at Falmouth and left on Saturday.

Our march on Friday was through the dust and up the Rappahannock on the main road toward Warrenton. The day was warm and we had, of course, clouds of dust. Encamped Friday evening at a creek. Had marched over twenty miles. We had marched in a circuitous route, probably to deceive the enemy, crossing the Aquia railroad at Stonemans Switch.

On Saturday we started early and rested frequently. The dust was intolerable at times. We arrived at Bealton Station, on the Orange & Alexandria R. R. in the afternoon. Then we turned to the left and went a mile. It looked like a move to Gordonsville, but it was only to get water, which was very scarce. We had a slight thunder shower on Saturday evening. It cooled the air and we rested comfortably.

On Sunday morning we started early. We were first drawn up in line of battle and ordered to load. There was a report that the enemy was crossing at a point west of Warrenton. We came along the Orange & Alexandria R. R. At noon we were at Warrenton Junction. There I saw John Crain, our cousin, who was well. He said the enemy was strong up the river. He had been in the cavalry fight. The march on Sunday morning was pleasant, but the sun came out at noon, and then it was hot and dusty. We marched until midnight, resting frequently. Our day's and night's march ended at Manasses Junction, where we rested till Monday, yesterday morning.

On Monday morning we resumed our march and came to Centreville. We got water and took lunch at Bull Run. We are now under orders and in readiness to move again. I do not know how far we are going today, but I presume not more than a few miles, unless it is the intention to go up to the right farther.

I am in fine health.

There is no use in commenting on the move nor on the results following Radical mismanagement. Six months since McClellan was removed, six months of blunder, disaster and defeat.

Camp near Broad Run, London Co., Va.,
Sunday, June 21, 1863.

My Dear Brother:

We are now lying at Broad Run, near London and Hampshire or Alexandria railroad. The First and Second Divisions are on the run below us. We are half a mile above the railroad. Leesburg is about ten miles distant. The Potomac at its nearest point is about five miles off. I presume you know the location pretty well. The Eleventh and Twelfth Corps are understood to be at Leesburg. The Fifth is on our left. The Third is at or near Centreville, and the rest somewhere else on the line between Centreville and Leesburg. From all the movements I presume it is intended to wait here for Lee to attack the whole army, which he will probably not do.

I have said the Twelfth Corps was at Leesburg, and I was so informed, but I think at least a large portion of that corps must be at Alexandria.

After arriving at Broad Run on Thursday I was made officer of picket and ordered to locate the line. My instructions from General Doubleday were very vague, but I rode over the country until I got the points in my head and then established the line. A heavy thunder storm came on while I was riding the line, and I got a complete wetting. It rained all Thursday night. I got good eating at Greenlus House, but I did not wish to sleep. On Friday morning very early we heard cannon firing in three directions. I thought the ball was opening, but the firing did not last long. Then I lay down on Greenlus' floor and slept like a top till the relief came out.

Yesterday, in consequence of the First and Second Divisions coming up, the picket line was thrown out farther. General Rowley went out to change it, and I went with him. We did not meet with any adventure. The picket line now extends from the Leesburg pike on the right, through ———— station on the railroad, and along the old Ox road to a point on Broad Run about a mile above our camp.

On Friday evening at 9 o'clock we got orders to pack up and move immediately. I was writing a note to my wife. It was raining heavily. Colonel Cummins and I concluded to avail ourselves of the last minute, and the order was soon countermanded, but the Second Brigade did not get the countermand, and their officers and men stood in line in a drenching rain until morning. It was a cruel blunder, but we see many such. Army life is not very pleasant at best, but our Generals by a want of reflection or interest in their commands make the service ten-fold more irksome than it should be. For instance, coming from Warrenton Junction to Manasses Junction over a plain road, we were marched four miles out of our way. This was on Sunday and it was a boiling hot day. To make up for it we had to march till midnight to reach Manasses Junction.

I have no idea what is coming. I thought when we

fell back that Lee had been heavily re-inforced, and that a big battle was certain, but it is by no means clear that our Generals have not been completely deceived.

Camp at Broad Run, London Co., Va.,
June 22, 1863.

My Dear Brother:

We are still at the same point where I wrote my last letter. We are lying at Broad Run on the east side of it near the railroad. The First Division is lying on our right at the railroad.

Yesterday there was heavy cannonading all day. We did not know what it meant. It seemed to be a heavy fight confined to one spot, and almost directly west. We had orders to pack up, and lay all day ready to move at a moment's notice. About 5 o'clock P. M. orders came to pitch tents, accompanied with news that the affair had been a cavalry fight at the Gap, near Aldie, and that our cavalry had driven the enemy. Probably the thing was a reconnoissance by Lee.

If Lee has as large an army as reported we will have a big fight soon. He is in a position to fight or retire at pleasure. I hardly think he meditates moving a large force into Pennsylvania. The Eleventh and Twelfth Corps are ahead of us, the former at Leesburg. The Fifth is at Goose Creek, also ahead of us. The rest of the army reaches to the Orange & Alexandria railroad. Hooker's headquarters are at Centreville.

The force around Washington in the fortifications is larger now than Hooker's army. I presume, as usual, on the event of a fight the main body of our army will be held in reserve too far off to do anything.

We get little news now. The papers are three days behind. I have read about the raid and the nomination of Judge.

The Radicals calculate that the raid will stimulate the war spirit and strengthen their party. I think it will be just the reverse. Nothing shows more conclusively the

incompetency of our men at Washington than the fact
that such raids can be made, and that with one army
larger than Lee's in their command they allow him to do
as he pleases.

I am very nearly out of patience. I can see no sign
of any change for the better. The President has 60,000
men in the defences and a whole corps at Baltimore and
scattered along the railroad (B. & V.). He could unite
these forces and sweep Lee's army out of existence, but
he will not do it. He will still hug the main body close
for personal protection and blame the *Copperheads* for
the result, because they have denounced the odious features of the conscription law, while he has made no sincere attempt to enforce it in time to meet the exigencies
of the service.

Much love to mother and all friends. I am in good
health. My clothes are nearly all worn out, and I look
very seedy. I am in good spirits. My personal relations
with General Rowley, an old acquaintance from Pittsburg, who commands the brigade; Colonel Biddle, Major
Biddle (One Hundred and Twenty-first), Colonel Dana,
of the One Hundred and Forty-third, and other officers,
are very agreeable. Colonel Dana is quite an accomplished gentleman, and a Democrat. The Biddles are
both good men. Colonel Allen is home on sick leave.
Dana is in Colonel Stone's brigade, the Second. Stone
is a humbug.

Middletown, Md.,
July 8, 1863.

My Dear Brother:

Arrived here at 10 A. M. this morning. Came yesterday from Emmettsburg to the foot of Kittochin Mountain on this side about four miles from here. It was a
weary march twenty-five miles. Have not time to write
much. First Corps in the advance; we are now encamped one mile southwest of town. The papers say
that Lee's retreat is cut off. I do not believe it. Things

do not look so, at any rate. I hear rumors that Lee has crossed near Williamsport with his entire force; and the appearance of the army and our movements indicate that such is the fact. Still I may be mistaken. I am in good health. It rained all this morning, and I am wet to the skin, but all right.

Camp near Boonsboro, Md.,
Thursday, July 9, 1863.

My Dear Brother:

You know all about the battle of Gettysburg. I need not repeat what I have written, nor what you have read in the papers.

On Monday morning the army was put in motion. I presume it was a day too late, but that is not so clear. The greatest generals in the world's estimation are the men who go for entire victory or complete defeat. Napoleon was one of them, and he closed his career at St. Helena, and suffered the worst rout that ever befel an army. We cannot afford such risks and our successes are correspondingly less decisive.

Our march on Monday morning lay over a part of the battlefield on the left for the distance of a mile or more. The ground was still marked with newly made graves, with the bloated and disgusting bodies of horses with their mouths open and eye-balls protruding. Many human bodies were still unburied and the faces were black and the teeth grinning horribly. The trees were shattered by shot and shell. Wheat fields were trodden down. War had done its work; and the air was terribly offensive with the odor of thousands of rotting bodies. It was a relief to reach the outside of the terrible scene, to come again among beautiful farms, and through fields of ripe grain, and at last to reach Emmettsburg, where I enjoyed a good supper with a gentleman named McBride, a Catholic, who treated me with great kindness. I sat down with him and his family with feelings of no common pleasure.

At Emmettsburg I procured several things which I needed much, including the stationery which I am now using. Our camp was near the village on the north side. We remained there until Tuesday morning. Early on Tuesday we started on the road to Frederick City, but turned to the right and crossed the mountain by way of a little old collection of log houses called Hamburg. The road was very narrow and steep. The scenery, of course, was wild enough. We marched about twenty-five miles that day, and encamped at the foot of the mountain (Kittochin) on this side four miles northeast of Middletown. A heavy rain came on just after we encamped. I slept in a hay-mow after getting a good supper at a farm house. It rained nearly all night.

Early on Wednesday morning we started again and marched to Middletown through a drenching rain. Last October our regiment marched through the same town with new clothes, new colors, and a fine band playing national airs. Then we had nine hundred men. Now we have less than a hundred, Colonel, Major, Adjutant, all gone. Then the people were waving flags and our men were cheering. Now the poor fellows left are too tired to raise more than a faint hurrah, and are tramping through the mud wet to the skin. "There is the house, Colonel, where they gave us apples." So they did eight months ago. A pretty girl distributed them. The pretty girl is at the window again, looking sadly at the jaded troops, and does not recognize the regiment, does not hear music, sees nothing but dirty, weary forms carrying two tattered flags, and going on, still going on to the end of the great journey.

We encamped a mile this side of Middletown. Orders were to pitch tents and stay all night. Our corps since leaving Gettysburg has been in the advance. I went back from camp to Middletown and got something to eat. The town was very lively. The rain had ceased. The Eleventh Corps was passing through. They are great on music, but poor on fighting. The truth must be told of that confounded corps. It is not worth a sixpence. One or two brigades in it are honorable exceptions. Had the Eleventh Corps done anything on the first we would have been as successful that day as on the second and third.

I took a room at a hotel and wrote a letter or two. I remained in town all afternoon, and troops were passing all the time. About sundown I started out to camp and took the wrong road. By this mistake I came upon the Pennsylvania Reserves and had a pleasant conversation with Major Knox and Colonel Fisher. I had a bottle of wine with me to contribute to the gaieties. Such hours of sunshine only come at long intervals in army life.

My pleasant chat was interrupted by the intelligence that the First Corps had suddenly moved. So I started to overtake the regiment. When I got on the right road it was twilight. My way lay up the mountain gap. Reno was killed on that mountain. The view of the valley is lovely at any time as you ascend at that point. The music of twenty bands was floating off in the evening air, and I listened to it till it was drowned in the sound of swollen mountain streams. The camp fires of fifty thousand troops over the valley looked like the gas lights of a large city. My ride was a long and weary one. It was 11 o'clock when I reached the point where our corps, which was drawn up in line of battle, lay near the road, but the regiment lay in a spot which is not very easy to reach in daylight and my horse was nearly done up. So I got a place to pasture him, and a farmer's wife gave me a pillow on the floor, and I slept comfortably till morning. It was told us last night that our cavalry and the enemy's had been fighting all day near Boonsboro, that Lee's army could not cross for want of bridges, and that another general battle was coming off soon. The cavalry fight was truth, but I think it was only Lee's rear guard.

I rose at daylight and came up to the regiment. It is lying on the side of the mountain in the woods. Soon after breakfast and as the fog cleared up there was rapid firing of musketry down at the foot of the mountain and near us, but we could see no enemy. Our men sat very coolly looking down, like birds on a perch, to ascertain the cause. A band was playing down there and teams were on the road, but still the firing continued, and we concluded that it was merely the advance of our line of skirmishers from the Eleventh Corps, or the cavalry on our left. I guess this opinion was correct. It is now about 4 o'clock in the afternoon. Some troops have come down the Boonsboro pike, and taken position below us in the valley. The skirmish firing ceased before noon. I have not heard a cannon to-day.

My opinion is that Lee has crossed. I believe he had at least one solid bridge at or near Williamsport which was never destroyed, but I presume the newspaper reports give a different idea. (I have just heard a cannon shot this minute. It is toward Williamsport, and at least six miles off.)

I think there will be no general engagement on this side of the river, but I am not infallible. I did not expect a great battle at Gettysburg. Still that was because I did not fully understand the topography of the country, and I thought Gettysburg was more distant than it is from the Potomac. You ought to visit the Gettysburg field; if you go to the Rebel side you will think their position was the better one; if you go to our side you will think ours is preferable. It was a very fair fight, and we were successful. The victory was a great one. I know it will not satisfy everybody, but what would such men say of Solferino, Majenta or Sebastopol.

We were beaten at Fredericksburg in December. Nobody has been able to say that it was not a Rebel victory, and yet we did not lose a cannon or withdraw a single battery twenty feet on Saturday, December 12. We lay in the same position from Saturday evening till Monday evening, and then withdrew without losing a gun, and yet we acknowledge that Lee is a general of some ability.

At Chancellorsville the line of our army was not changed after Saturday night. We did not recross the river until Tuesday morning, and yet it was a Rebel victory and Lee is not denounced. Why cannot we do our own generals the same justice? Bagging an army is popular among men who know nothing about war, and care little about participating in its verities.

I am in good health. I have a vague hope that the trials and labors of our regiment are nearly over. We have less than a hundred men left. We lost over two-thirds of the force in action. A list of the killed, wounded and missing is in the Inquirer. I furnished it, but the names are badly printed.

Charley Connely is well. He is a fine, manly fellow, and well liked by his officers. Love to all friends.

Tell mother I hope we are nearly through and that I shall see her again.

Camp near Hagerstown, Md.,
July 10, 1863.

My Dear Brother:

I wrote you a long letter yesterday, and left it at Boonsboro to-day as we came through. Probably this one will reach you first. We were encamped last night near the foot of South Mountain, above Boonsboro. This morning early we heard cannon firing toward Hagerstown, and about the same time our corps took up the line of march in this direction. My horse is pretty nearly done out. The boys made his back sore, and he is in need of shoeing. I had to walk to-day nearly all the way. A servant (colored) took my other horse at Gettysburg to ride back for feed to the wagon train, and sold the horse. At any rate, he was seen walking, and, when asked what he had done with the horse, said he had left him with me. To add to my inconvenience a mule which I use to carry a tent, fly and eatables, got a sore back, and to-day it and the boy in charge of it have failed to keep up with the troops. I presume I shall never see boy, nor mule, nor fly, nor eatables.

This is a burning hot afternoon. The firing which was quite brisk nearly all day in front has ceased. Our army is very strong, and if we have a general engagement I

feel quite confident about the result, but I do not think
there will be a general battle.   I believe Lee is crossing
at Williamsport.

Berlin, Md.,
Saturday, July 18, 1863.

My Dear Brother:

On Thursday at Burkettsville my horse fell on me and
sprained my ankle.   The injury is not very severe nor
dangerous.   My right knee is also bruised some.   The
pain, however, was so intense that I could not ride in an
ambulance, and I made an application to be sent to the
general hospital.   I am now under orders to report to the
Medical Director at Georgetown, D. C.   If my leg is not
entirely well before a week I will probably get a leave
of absence.

I have to wait here a few hours for a train of cars.   I
am sitting in the telegraph office, and I cannot employ
the time better than by summing up the events of the
week.

I believe I wrote to you from a camp near Boonsboro
on Saturday or Sunday.   Well, we did not stay there
long.   Sunday forenoon was lovely.   It was quiet everywhere.   Even the army seemed to be reposing, and the
harvest fields were lying untouched, but our rest was
very short.   A thunderstorm was coming up.   We had
orders to move, and soon started toward Funkstown.
There was some discussion whether the distant thunder
was artillery, but a heavy rain soon settled the question.
I got completely wet to the skin.   Even my boots were
full of water.   We crossed Antietam creek and marched
down to the left about a mile.   There we were formed
in line of battle, and to our surprise found ourselves under the occasional fire of the enemy's sharpshooters and
skirmishers.   The firing soon became very brisk and
finally our men drove the enemy's skirmishers and pickets
back about half a mile.   We then perceived our real po-

sition. We were in the front line and the enemy's line of entrenchments was plainly seen about a mile distant along the edge of the woods.

The skirmishing continued all evening. We expected a battle soon. I lay down without a tent in the rain on a sheaf of wheat. It was a damp bed, but I slept soundly till 1 or 2 o'clock. Then I got up and rekindled a dying fire and slept beside it till daylight.

Our men immediately after forming their line commenced throwing up a rude breastwork of rails and earth. Both armies now use the spade. The Rebel entrenchments at Gettysburg are very strong. One man behind such defences is as good as two outside. Some of our commanders are all for high chivalry. At Gettysburg, instead of taking advantage of a fence which happened to be just in the right place, we got an order to charge bayonet against a double line of infantry twice as strong as our own. Some very brave and high-toned officers lack discretion.

On Monday morning we were secure from an attack and ready to make one. The day was cool and cloudy. Hour after hour passed on, however, and still nothing was done, but a little skirmishing. We listened for the opening of artillery on the right or left, but not a gun was heard. Bye and bye came a report that Senator Somebody and the Vice President were in the neighborhood. Along with it came the intelligence that Lee had been strongly re-inforced, that Beauregard had joined him with 40,000 men. I am half inclined to believe that this unfounded rumor came from a high source, and that the loss of the golden opportunity will yet be traced to the common origin of blunders.

Looking back we can see that that one day's delay was an error, but it was by no means palpable at the time. Lee's army was entrenched. It occupied a strong, natural position, the dividing ridge between the Potomac and Antietam creek. The streams run nearly parallel. It is by no means certain that we would have carried the line at the first assault. Another supposition was, that Lee had no means of crossing, and was compelled to make a desperate resistance. If so the work before us was no child's play, and delay was by no means dangerous or impolitic. Although I would much prefer seeing McClellan in command of this army, I thing it would be unjust to set General Meade's error down as a blunder. He is a brave man, and did a great work at Gettysburg. For that alone he deserves the gratitude of the people for all time.

On Monday afternoon the battery of the enemy directly in front of us fired three or four shells. We thought the ball had opened in earnest. Our batteries, however, did not reply, and evening came on without anything being accomplished. I slept under a shelter tent that night very comfortably. We had some expectation that the fight would commence early, but on awaking the first rumor I heard was that the enemy had gone. Presently a prisoner was brought in. He had not awakened in time, and missed the move. After a few minutes a young farmer came past, and said he had been cooped inside of the Rebel lines for several days, but that they sloped during the night. He looked like an uncaged bird. He was making tracks for a neighbor's house to carry the good news—good news to people who in the event of a fight would have participated in its terrors and suffering.

On Tuesday before noon we started toward Williamsport. We soon crossed the Rebel entrenchments. The position was admirably selected and well improved. As we glanced at the works in passing some of us could not help a quiet self-congratulation that we had been spared the trouble of an assault.

We encamped on Tuesday evening near Williamsport. It rained again. I rode into town and saw where a part of the Rebels had crossed.

Wednesday was a bright and warm day. We started early and marched more than twenty miles. I got a good dinner at a farm house, taking pot luck with half a dozen men who were harvesting. We crossed Antietam creek a short distance above the old battlefield, passed through Keidysville and Rohersville, and encamped for the night about a mile from the place where I passed a miserable night last fall. The day's march was severe on the men; several died of sunstroke.

Early on Thursday we resumed our march toward this place. Passing through Burkettsville my horse, a borrowed one, became unruly. He is a vicious brute. He finally reared and fell backward with my right leg under him. I held his head down until I got my foot free, and then let him get up. I found that my leg was somewhat bruised and my ankle sprained. A farmer allowed me to occupy a room in his house until an ambulance came up. I then enjoyed my first ride in one of those delightful vehicles. It is comparable to nothing but a trip over Sandy Hill in the Butler hack.

I owe my misfortune to a faithless nigger. It was my luck to have in my employ at Gettysburg an African with a hangdog look. I gave him my brown horse to go back to the wagon train. When he reached the train the horse was not with him. On being interrogated by the other boys he said that he left the horse with me. He also showed a considerable sum of money to one of them. After this act of embezzlement he sloped toward Baltimore. I may meet him yet. At times in my dreams I imagine myself giving up my commission and devoting myself to the task of bringing the fellow to justice. The loss of my horse compelled me to borrow another, for I had to use one to carry blankets and feed. The animal which I got was a vicious brute and full of tricks.

We encamped on Thursday evening about three miles from Berlin. It rained all night. I lay in the tent all day yesterday. It was a wet, dreary day. My order to report to Georgetown arrived in the evening, and I came over to this place in an ambulance. We were delayed several hours by wagons.

This morning our whole corps passed and crossed the river on the pontoon bridge at the same place we crossed last fall.

I saw Hoover Shannon, George Plumer, George Snowden, Captain Gray, Charley Connely and everybody else as they passed along the street an hour ago. They were all well. They all had a kind word to say to me, and generally congratulated me on my accident. It is a sad fact that the privations and hardships of army life are so severe that sickness or the loss of a limb is regarded as a blessing rather than a calamity. I am free to confess that the prospect of a week's repose, of getting clean clothes, and of seeing friends again more than compensates for the pain I have suffered and am likely to suffer from a sprained ankle.

I believe the war is nearly over. I doubt much whether there will be any battle in Virginia soon, if at all.

Camp at Rappahannock Station,
Friday, Sept. 4, 1863.

My Dear Brother:

I received a very interesting letter from you yesterday. It enclosed a puff in the "Monitor." I am sorry the writer reflected on the editor of the "Register," who has always done me full justice, and is, I believe, personally friendly to me. Beside, the puff itself is in bad taste, very much overdone and calculated to do a man more harm than good. But I do not care much for such things. If I can get back into civil life again with a sound constitution and without positive disgrace, I shall be contented. I am almost indifferent to newspaper blame or approbation, because I helped to edit one a number of years, and know how little there is of true value in anything they say. There used to be a set of men about Pittsburg who had to be puffed about once a month. The thing was essential to their happiness. They expected it regularly. If you omitted any opportunity of bringing their names forward they would call and complain about it. Some of them were so considerate as to write their own notes. They, without an exception, I believe, all attained pretty high political positions. Some are dead and some hold their places still. It would amuse you to take up an old file of newspapers and read the different notices of distinguished men, provided the editor for the time could sit beside you and explain the circumstances under which they were written.

We have not moved since I wrote last. We have an occasional rumor of Rebel demonstrations, and then we get orders to be ready to fall in and march on short notice, but everything goes on as if we were here for an indefinite period. They dig wells everywhere by blasting the rock. The occasional explosions sound like artillery, and sometimes occasion reports of imaginary movements.

We get mails regularly, and every afternoon we receive the morning papers of that day. The cars come to Bealton station, four miles back, but the locomotive runs up to this point two or three times a day to get water. When it comes in it whistles loud enough to make the Rebels believe that we are getting recruits by the thousand.

Our regiment is filling up slowly with arrivals from convalescent camp. Several men wounded at Gettysburg have returned. One sergeant, who was shot in the mouth, has the appearance of a man with a hare lip. We have now about one hundred and forty men present for duty. We have not yet received any drafted men.

Our men are doing picket duty across the river. We send out about one-half of those present every two days. They remain out until relieved, forty-eight hours. The number left in camp is too small for battalion drill, and accordingly we do nothing but smoke and read newspapers when they come.

The men have arbors built over their shelter tents. The camps are rather neat. Those of the Pennsylvania Reserves are near us and in sight. Colonel Knox called on Wednesday. He is in good health and spirits.

Some nervous anxiety seems to be felt just now about Lee's movements. It is undoubtedly true that this army has been weakened since we left Williamsport. If Lee has been strengthened and should assume the offensive we will have to fall back. Should this occur soon it will cast a damper over the whole country. It would be a much wiser policy to withdraw the army before an attack is actually made.

My command is so small now that it seems almost ridiculous to call it a regiment, but it will become larger if we do not get into another fight. One more battle would nearly wipe it out of existence.

I have been recommended for promotion to the office of Colonel. The papers went up to Governor Curtin two weeks ago, but he has not seen proper to act on them. If I cannot be promoted I shall resign. I will not submit to injustice.

I cannot give up my political opinions to gain a position to which I am entitled in the regular order of military promotion, and I presume Governor Curtin would not think of requiring such terms. But more than that I cannot afford to write to him and importune him for this thing as a personal favor. I believe I have a right to it, and if he and others cannot see the matter in that light I can afford to resign. Our Adjutant was a nephew of the Governor. When he fell at Gettysburg mortally wounded, I helped him to rise, and with the aid of one of the men carried him back to the seminary, where he died. Had I not done so he would have perished on the field, for all our troops had fallen back and he and I were several paces in the rear. Under the circumstances, I should not like to solicit my promotion as a favor, nor have any of my friends take any steps to procure it. But there is no use in saying anything about this matter now. I presume the commission will come in due time. If it does not I can resign.

The weather has become very cool and pleasant. We require blankets at night. We get soft bread and fresh beef now all the time. The commissary supplies are our chief dependence. We can buy nothing in the country. It is very thinly settled in this locality, and the few people who live here are very poor. Sutlers bring us a few luxuries at fearful prices. On the whole we are not suffering.

The men have had a rough time of it. Those of my regiment have all used more clothing than their allowance. This had been in consequence of the hard marches.

They are all in debt. Troops that lay around Washington can save money on their clothing accounts. So the thing works. The harder the service the less the pay.

Camp near Raccoon Ford, Va.,
Sept. 28, 1863.

My Dear Brother:

I forgot the date of my last letter to you, but I believe it was written at camp near Culpeper, C. H. Well, we left it on Thursday last and marched down through the pine woods to a point about two miles from Mitchell's Ford. There we remained until yesterday (Sunday) afternoon. Our stay at that place was only marked by the execution of a deserter. It was a sad sight. They shot five a week ago in the Fifth Corps, but there is something far more impressive in the fate of a single man than in the destruction of a hundred. Whatley's rhetoric contains a strong chapter based on this idea. He shows the true philosophy of the excitement of sensibilities.

The deserter who suffered behaved very courageously. He marched steadily around the field, keeping step to the mournful music of the band. Then his spiritual adviser prayed with him a long time, and after that he stood up firmly to be shot, and fell over his coffin without a struggle. One bullet passed through his head and another through his heart. The troops had to pass the body marching as if in review in column of companies. Then the bands struck up "The Red, White and Blue," and the ceremony was over.

On the morning that we left Culpeper encampment, General Kenley proved to be in liquor. The corps commander put him under arrest. General Rowley is also under arrest for the same offence. The accident of these two Brigadiers being suspected of taking too much whisky places Colonel Chapman Biddle in command of the Third Division, and gives me the command of our brigade. I find one advantage in the position, that I have always good quarters. To-night, for instance, I have a wall tent to myself, a snug bed, and a fine blazing fire out in front. It needs all these luxuries to make the place cheerful. We are in a dismal spot. The woods are partly pine and partly oak, and very dense. Our encampment is on a small farm or clearing of some forty acres in the middle of what the owner supposed to be an impenetrable wilderness. Poor man. His fences are all gone, and his few cows and pigs are sharing the same fate. However, it may be all for the best. He will be compelled to leave this region, and he will learn what he would not otherwise have discovered—that there is a better country out west.

We are not far from the Rapidan, perhaps a mile or two. The enemy has fortified the opposite bank. I believe we are in reach of his guns, but there is no firing now, and there has been none for several days. It is not easy to say what we are going to do. It is reported that one corps of our army has gone back. If so I think we are not going to cross the Rapidan. It seems to me that if we had been going over at all the crossing would have been made a week ago.

I have given my promotion up. I could not be mustered in without more men, and it seems we are not going to get any.

I perceive by the papers that you are in a political war almost as annoying as a regular military campaign. There is no such thing as peace any place this side of heaven, and we read that there was once war there, too. It may be my luck to have it break out again if I should ever get there. I am tired of the thing, so is everybody else. A victory only prolongs the strife, for our rulers do not know how to use an advantage when they have it. They will not treat when they are successful, and when they meet reverses they cannot.

Camp, near Raccoon Ford,
Sunday, Oct. 4, 1863.

My Dear Brother:

Gen. Kenley was released from arrest yesterday, and returned to his command of the 3rd division. Biddle returned to the brigade, and I abdicated in his favor. I enjoyed the command about a week. Our brigade is a very interesting feature of the army. It numbers about three hundred and fifty men for duty. Col. Dana commanding the 143rd, has received a full complement of conscripts, and in consequence his regiment is about three times as large as our brigade. I do not understand why neither the 121st nor the 142nd received any drafted men. but I am not very anxious about getting them. They would give me a great deal of trouble, and on the whole it is perhaps as well to be without them. Curtin pays no attention to my recommendations for the promotion of line officers. I presume he is aware that I am not politically in his favor.

We are lying about a mile and a half from Raccoon Ford on the Culpeper Court House road. On Thursday I was Corps officer of the picket, and rode the line along the river. It is nearly seven miles long and connects on the right with the pickets of the 2nd corps. The country along the river is beautiful.

I see no signs of an immediate forward movement. The withdrawal of the 11th and 12th corps would look like abandonment of the onward movement. Our eight day ration order has been countermanded, and we now have only three days' rations on hand. On Friday it rained very hard all day and all night. My tent was filled with water. The ground here is level and swampy. I presume the roads are now in such a condition that moving would be difficult even if it had been determined on, but everything indicates an abandonment of the March to Richmond.

Half a dozen cannon shots have just been fired at the Ford. We do not know the cause yet. 10 o'clock A. M.

Camp on Culpeper C. H. Road,
near Raccoon Ford,
Oct. 6, 1863.

My Dear Brother:

Just as I was closing a letter to you on Sunday we heard several cannon shots down at the river. We had instantly orders to be under arms, and I closed my letter and put it in the mail. In about half an hour we had an explanation of the cause of the firing. A small party with a wagon were foraging near the river, and the Rebels opened on them, firing half a dozen shells without doing any damage. There the matter ended. We soon received orders, however, to change our camp for other reasons. Some guerillas had been prowling around the artillery batteries and had captured one man. Our little brigade was accordingly moved to a point on the Culpeper road about half a mile from our last camp, and farther from the river, where we are now lying. While we were in the act of moving Colonel Knox called, and he remained with me during the whole of Sunday afternoon. Coop. Cochran was with him.

We now have a very pleasant camp, with a pretty good view of surrounding country, and of the Blue Ridge range in the distance. We have good water and plenty of rails for fuel. The nights are cold. Very soon stoves or fire-places will be a necessity. It is coming near the season when military movements in this locality will be attended with great difficulty. I shall not be surprised if our army is withdrawn beyond the Rappahannock, or even to the defences at Washington. The intention undoubtedly was to proceed toward Richmond by this route, but two weeks ago a change was perceptible. The day on which we left Culpeper C. H. I saw a general order at army headquarters for all teams to be held in readiness to move to the rear on short notice. Knox says it had been decided then at Washington to make a retrograde movement, but the order was changed, and only two corps, the Eleventh and Twelfth, were taken away to reinforce Rosecrantz. The withdrawal of these two corps has reduced the army so much that I believe no onward movement is contemplated just now, and it will very soon be too late to attempt it. Some pretty shrewd observers say that we are all going to fall back, and that the movement is only delayed in consequence of the approaching election. If the army were to retreat now it would very probably injure the Republican cause.

I have very little hope of Woodward's election, but I could almost pray for it. Something is wanted to rebuke the Radicals, or they will persist in an eternal war. I observe a good sign of returning common sense at Washington in the speech of the Postmaster General. But the trouble with our rulers is that they are never conservative at the right time. It requires a defeat to make them talk moderation. In the hour of success they become extravagant in their demands, and lose the favorable opportunity for restoring peace. I wish I could have been at home to take the stump for Woodward, but neither my vote nor my exertions could change the result.

Captain William Hasson has resigned and been discharged honorably. I strained a point and recommended the acceptance of his resignation *for the benefit* of the service. His business was suffering in his absence, and he had apprehension of being utterly ruined, though he owns a very productive oil interest. There seemed to be no way to save him but to certify as I did. There is something very arbitrary and tyrannical in the position assumed at Washington, that an officer cannot resign, but that the President can dismiss one at pleasure. The true doctrine I think was laid down by Justice McLean, of the United States Supreme Court, that the right of resignation is an incident to every office, civil or military. The President undoubtedly can remove any military officer at pleasure. He exercises this right very often, but his power to do so implies the officer's right to resign.

George Snowden is now entitled to be Captain of Company I, and I shall send up a recommendation immediately, but I presume it will be treated with silent contempt like all my former recommendations.

The weather is clear and nights very cold. The railroad is about three or four miles off, and we are pretty well supplied. Captain Over, of the Tenth Reserves, and William Kennedy, Lieutenant in the Sixteenth Cavalry, called to-day and took dinner with me. They were both in good health and spirits. The Sixteenth Cavalry is now lying back at Bealton station. These officers represent that the opinion in favor of a backward movement is very general.

Camp at Thoroughfare Gap, Va.,
Friday, Oct. 23, 1863.

My Dear Brother:

I have had very poor conveniences for writing during the last two weeks. Even now I have nothing but a fly over me, and it is too cold to give you a long letter. The First Corps is at this point on the west side of the mountain. As you will see by the map we are on the Manasses Gap railroad. A train of cars came up to-day. It was the first on this route for a long time. It took some sick men back toward Washington on its return.

We have had a rough time of it in marching, exposure and hardships since leaving Raccoon Ford, but we have seen very little fighting. The suspense, however, was constant for two weeks. I will have to refer you to my letters to my wife for particulars.

We now understand that the enemy has re-crossed the Rappahannock. I think the probabilities are that there will be no general engagement in this department. The weather will soon stop operations.

We have been lying here three days. There are no signs of moving immediately. Of course, I cannot tell what will be done. Perhaps we may go to work to build bridges, and reconstruct the Gordonsville railroad, and try to re-occupy the ground voluntarily abandoned. I confess my inability to see through the stupendous plans of Hallock & Co. I hope I shall live to learn who was the mighty individual who has directed the movements of this army since McClellan was removed.

Rosencrantz has fallen, too. It seems he was a terrible man. He ate opium, drank whisky, was drunk at

Chattanooga during the great battle, is suspected of disloyalty, etc. etc. It is strange that all this has been discovered since the election.

I am still in good health, but somewhat tired and disgusted. When we get settled I shall apply for a short leave of absence, but some new scheme may put us in motion for a winter campaign.

Camp at Briston Station, Va.,
Thursday, Oct. 29, 1863.

My Dear Brother:

I believe my last letter to you was written at Thoroughfare Gap. Our corps left that point on Saturday last, and we had a cold and wet march to this place, which we reached after dark. Briston station, as you know, is on the Orange & Alexandria railroad, about three miles southwest of Manasses Junction. We seem to be employed in guarding the railroad. The main body of the army is in front at Warrenton, Warrenton Junction and other points. The enemy is still reported as having some force on this side of the Rappahannock. We have a strong force of engineers and laborers repairing the road which was completely destroyed beyond this point. What we will do when the work is finished is hard to tell, for it is certain we accomplished nothing when we had it in perfect working order. I presume it is deemed necessary to keep up a show of activity, and to menace the enemy in this direction, but the probability of reaching Richmond or even Gordonsville by this route at this season is one of a very remote order.

The extreme sensitiveness of our people at Washington concerning the safety of the capitol has been the source of innumerable blunders. They allow it to frustrate every plan. Lee understands them perfectly, and he only finds it necessary now to make a feint of moving on Washington to put our whole army on the right about at double quick.

It is not very easy to see the sagacity or military strategy of our recent retreat. Nor is our present advance a

5

manifest masterstroke. The withdrawal of McClellan's
army from Richmond instead of re-inforcing it was a
still more palpable blunder. And yet it is strange that,
in spite of errors innumerable, we gain a little gradually.
Still one gets sick at heart at the prospect of an intermin-
able war. Probably the effect of all these mistakes in
policy will be to make the result finally depend on the respective resources and powers of endurance of the two
parties. I am not quite sure that, laying foreign interference out of the question, our true policy would not be
to hold our positions in the different states, maintain the
blockade and never risk a battle without almost a certainty of success. Our people at the North are very
tired of the war. The army is very tired, and I presume
the southern people and army are suffering far more
than ours.

I am only writing this twaddle because I have nothing else.

We are lying in a very pleasant spot where the railroad
crosses Broad run. I have got a flue in my tent and am
quite comfortable. Our company has received soft bread,
beans and molasses, and we are contemplating a fine
dinner. We have lived on crackers and poor beef or
ham for three weeks.

I am pretty well tired of the service. My regiment
numbers 160 for duty. I cannot be promoted. It seems
absurd in every point of view to be signing papers, making requisitions, having battalion drills, and going
through the motions in general with little more than a
company. Colonel Biddle commands the First Brigade,
including our regiment and his own. The brigade numbers a little over three hundred men for duty. He is
heartily disgusted with the service, and has tendered his
resignation. He is a very correct man, and a fine officer. He attends particularly to the most minute duty.
He is always at his post and on hand for business. It is
painful to see such a man under the command of one
every way his inferior, a monkey-faced individual, who
is drunk two-thirds of the time, and incompetent when
he is sober.

General Rowley has procured a nice berth. All goes

by political and personal favoritism. Rowley has been ordered to Portland, Maine. He was under arrest, but that made no difference. He is to superintend the draft.

A regular Brigadier General is not often seen in the army. Brigades are commanded by Colonels. There are, you know, a great many Brigadiers, but they were nearly all appointed from improper influences, and the same influences are equally potent to secure them comfortable quarters at a distance from the field.

The weather is getting cold and reminds one of the severities of camp life and marches that we suffered a year ago. Even now our movements are attended with many hardships. The poor men have a hard time of it.

Camp near Catlett's Station, Va.
Nov. 21, 1863.

My Dear Brother:

I presume by this time you have arrived at home. I was somewhat disappointed that you did not visit the army. You could have enjoyed comfortable quarters and good fare in the same neighborhood where your regiment lay in the spring of 1862. Your friend, Dr. Edmonds, gave us,—i. e., our field and staff,—a good dinner the other day. His father-in-law, Stone, talks like a good Union man, and seems to enjoy some special privileges. For instance, yesterday he got a pass to visit Alexandria and buy some necessaries for his family.

A few days since we received orders to be ready to march on short notice, but present indications are that our division will be left here to guard the railroad. Several orders which have been received by the rest of the army in relation to baggage foreshadowing warm work in front, and a rapid advance have not been extended to us. I understand that the troops have been required to send back their knapsacks. I can hardly believe it. But one thing is certain, that no matter how light the trains may be there will be some difficulty in advancing. It has rained steadily all day with no sign of abatement.

The country along the Rapidian is very swampy, and I do not see how artillery is to be moved in that region at this season. Still it is clear that Gen. Meade is going to try something. It is probable that the army is on the move already.

The news from Tennessee is rather discouraging. It is not easy after one has seen something of the service to perceive the advantage of retrograde movements unless they are the result of compulsion. A retreat is very demoralizing on the men and dispiriting to the country.

We get the papers here regularly and enjoy many of the luxuries and comforts of civil life, but we have no danger of forgetting that we are in military service. Every day the Guerillas appear in our vicinity in small parties and pick up any unfortunate fellow who may be wandering off by himself. We have not yet lost any men. This regiment has the responsibility of guarding about four miles of road and taking care of itself at the same time. As we have only two hundred men and but 176 armed, the labor is more than we can do properly. I only hope that nothing like a raid will be made on us, for if it should be, our force will not be adequate to prevent depredations. I have thrown up rifle pits all around our camp and converted the old stable and other buildings into block houses, but I doubt if my engineering would receive much praise at the hands of military men. It is more probably of the kind called *civil*.

Major Kennedy and his brother spent the night here not long since and gave me some of the Franklin news. According to all reports the little village is improving at a rapid rate.

Camp near Catlett's Station, Va.
Dec. 3, 1863, Thursday.

My Dear Brother:

After a week of suspense occasioned by the peculiar movements in front we learn this morning that the army is falling back and that the head quarters of Gen. Meade are at Brandy station, five miles beyond the Rappahannock. As there has been no cannonading heard for two days, I presume the retrograde movement was a result of a conviction that the Confederate works at Orange Court House and the position of the army at that point were too strong to be taken without a ruinous sacrifice. At any rate our advance stopped on Monday, and now we have the retreat announced as a certainty. From the sound of the firing on Friday, Saturday and Sunday, I supposed there was a severe battle, but it turns out that the loss on both sides was very small. I had very little hope that the movement would be a success. Meade's army is not very large, and the roads on the Rapidan must be in a miserable condition, freezing at night and thawing by day. This disadvantage to the attacking party is almost insurmountable. If Meade draws off his forces without loss he will have accomplished a good purpose, for his movement has doubtless prevented the reinforcement of the armies of Bragg and Longstreet.

We are still encamped near Edmond's house, and my headquarters are in the house of Mr. Peters. I have been under roof more than three weeks.

On Monday we lost one of our men. He had gone out without leave to get wood, and was chopping with his rifle near him. Another man, unarmed, was carrying the wood. The latter saw three men dressed in blue overcoats seize the man who was chopping. They took him about a mile and a half. A party was sent in pursuit. They heard a shot fired, and upon going forward, found the dead body of our man in the pine woods. It was a cruel and cowardly murder. The poor fellow was a mere boy. The perpetrators of this outrage belonged to Moseby's gang.

I cannot be mustered in as Colonel, not having eight

hundred and thirty men on my rolls. There is no probability that I ever will have that number. I am in good health. I read the Spectator puff.

                              Camp near Paoli Mills, Va,
                                  Tuesday, Dec. 8, 1863.
My Dear Brother:
    We arrived at this point day before yesterday. Our camp is near Mountain Run, about five miles from Rappahannock station, and about three or four miles southeast from Brandy station. The distance to Kelly's Ford is about the same. The remainder of our corps is in the same neighborhood. We were relieved by the 5th corps Saturday afternoon, and left Catlett's station before sundown. That evening we came to Licking Run, a few miles this side of Warrenton Junction. On Sunday forenoon we finished our march, and we are now occupying a lot of cabins which were built by the Rebels for winter quarters. They are very snug and comfortable. We see no very great indications of a battle. I presume there will be none, unless Lee, when reinforced by Longstreet, should assume the offensive. Our army is all on the north side of Mountain Run. We have no news of the Rebels being in great force this side of the Rapidan.
    I saw Col. Knox at Catletts. He was expecting to leave for home soon. His resignation has been accepted.
    I am in good health, but feel a little depressed at the prospect of remaining all winter away down here without seeing home. The weather is clear and cold, but the mud will be terrible as soon as we have rain or snow.
    I have not been mustered in as Colonel, and I presume will not be. Capt. McClure, an old friend of mine from Carlisle, thought it of sufficient importance to send me a verbal message to the effect that my name had been mentioned favorably in Gen. Doubleday's report of the battle of Gettysburg.
    Col. Chapman Biddle has resigned. His papers went

forward yesterday. I presume he has influence sufficient at Washington to secure his escape from the service. He is a good officer, and a brave man, but he is
very anxious to leave. If the Colonel leaves I will probably be in command of the Brigade, but there will be
very little advantage in the position.

I am glad to hear that Franklin is prospering. I hope
I shall live to see it in its good days, and to meet my old
friends again, but it is hard to see a clear place in the future.

Give my love to mother. It seems a long time since I
saw her. Perhaps I may get a leave of absence this
winter for a few days and visit you, but I must wait until
the army gets settled in winter quarters.

Camp near Paoli Mills, Va.
Dec. 19, 1863.

My Dear Brother:

I received yours of the 14th yesterday evening. Our
mail arrangements are pretty good when one can get
news from Franklin in four days.

Your offer is a very kind one. I mean your proposal
to work for my promotion, but I have not the most remote hope that you will be able to accomplish it. I have
not yet been mustered in as Colonel, and cannot be under
existing orders until I have eight hundred and thirty
men in my regiment. Perhaps our ranks may be filled up
with recruits in the spring, but unless the next draft
proves more successful than the last one I will not be
able to get enough men to bring my command up to the
minimum, (830). So you see here is a pretty long step at
the outset. Next we have in this division six colonels,
who rank me. It is true, I am the senior officer in this
brigade, and so have command of it, but there are only
two regiments in it (121st and 142d), and it is so small
that it will probably be consolidated with some other.

There will probably be but few Brigadiers appointed
and the selections must be made from a long list of ap-

plicants. It is no sham modesty which makes me acknowledge that there will be many disappointed who deserve the advancement and who will fill the position better than myself. To say nothing of our politics I think the foregoing considerations are sufficient to render my prospect of elevation very distant. I believe the most I can possibly expect is to be mustered in as Colonel. To accomplish that end it may be necessary to procure the repeal of an unjust act of congress (Act of March 3, 1863), which virtually stops all promotion in regiments that have been so unfortunate as to get into a fight. If I could be mustered to date back to my commission (July 4, 1863) I would gain about two hundred dollars in pay. Just now the money would be acceptable.

We are becoming quite reconciled to our new location. We hear rumors of another move backwards. The knowing ones say that we are to recross the Rappahannock on account of bad roads and difficulty of transporting supplies. The news is not particularly pleasant, for the men are all in pretty comfortable quarters here, and if we go back we may be put in some place almost destitute of timber.

I got a stove yesterday, and have it now in operation. The position of brigade commander enables me to have more comforts than I enjoyed last winter. Whether we are on a march or in camp, I can now have a wall tent for my own use, and the men are always very ready to do anything to oblige me.

Col. Chapman Biddle's resignation was accepted about a week ago, so that my position is secure as long as the brigade is organized as it is now, but we may be thrown into a connection with some other regiment with a live colonel in it, and then I can take up the lament of Wolsey.

I forget what there was in my last letter to convey the impression that I was in low spirits. I presume I expressed some dissatisfaction about my inability to be mustered, and I confess it is some what discouraging to reflect that I cannot have any promotion under existing orders and acts of congress. Perhaps, too, I may have complained of our dismal locality, but these matters do not disturb me much nor give me any great annoyance. I am generally very cheerful. My health is always good, I have a good appetite, and our fare is not of the worst. I sleep as soundly as ever, except that I have become so accustomed to be wakened by orders, that I jump instinctively the moment an orderly knocks at the tent door.

George Snowden, who is at home on a leave, will be able to tell you more than I can write about our condition, and prospects, but he is not very talkative, and perhaps you will not see him very often.

Leaves of absence are now granted on a regular system by general orders, but there is a provision in them that not more than one brigade commander shall be absent in a corps at the same time. I intend to apply for a leave as soon as I can see an opportunity. Should I succeed we can talk over everything. I find that I am entitled to a month's pay from the state while recruiting, prior to the organization of the regiment. I want to make a regular application for it. I can do this if I go home on leave, or can prepare the necessary papers here. But it will be more readily accomplished at Harrisburg.

We are on very light duty here. We furnish a daily detail of twenty men for picket. It is too muddy for drill, and the men have an easy time of it. The reserves who relieved us have more trouble than we had guarding the railroad. On the whole our present condition is about as good as army life can be made in Virginia waste with mud knee deep.

Butler, Pa.
Jan. 7, 1864, *Thursday.*

My Dear Brother:

I think I will not be able to visit you, and I am very sorry for it. I might leave to-morrow at noon and reach Franklin the next (Saturday) morning, but then I would have to go right on without being able to say more than "how are you?" and "good bye!"

But there is another difficulty. I have some business in Harrisburg. I wish to get some officers appointed, and to present a claim against the state for one month's pay while recruiting. The claim is, I believe, good, and I need the money.

My visit has been very pleasant, although I was unfortunate in not receiving any pay at Washington, and I lost time by the detention of the cars. My time with my family has been necessarily shortened. My leave expires on the 10th. As you very justly said, a ten days' leave is too short for men in Western Pennsylvania.

Tell mother I am sorry I could not see her. My poor little toads look so lonely in this dreary town with its old snow covered roofs that it seems cruel to leave them until the very last minute. They are all in good health, and are very comfortable. Mr. Lowry's people are very kind to them. His house is quiet and well conducted. There is no noise or rowdyism about it.

Perhaps the war will end before long and then we can all be together again, but I confess I cannot see a very brilliant prospect of peace.

Camp, near Culpeper C. H., Va.
Monday, Jan. 18, 1864.

My Dear Brother:

This is a rainy day. The mud is pretty deep and getting deeper. I am confined to my quarters by the dreary aspect of things out of doors, and by an order for inspection, which will probably not be executed on account of the weather, but which, nevertheless, compels us to be in readiness for the brigade inspector.

Will Stehley is still with me. The order detailing him protects him from any charge of negligence while he is here. His regiment is now engaged in picket duty on the Rapidan. The Rebels fire on them occasionally. This fact and the bad weather make it very desirable for Will to remain where he is for the present. He sleeps in my tent and eats in my mess at present, but if he remains with me he will put up quarters of his own.

The two Biddles, Chapman and Alexander, in the 121st have both resigned and gone home. Capt. Lloyd of that regiment is entitled to be promoted as Lieut. Col., being the Senior line officer, but Biddle threw his influence in favor of the Adjutant, and it is said he will be appointed, though not in the line of promotion at all. Col. Biddle had some singular notions considering his industry in studying tactics and army regulations. He maintained that an adjutant could command a regiment if he was the senior officer. Accordingly Lt. Gray, of Venango, who was the senior line officer last summer, had to yield to Adjutant Hall, who was not a line officer and never had been, but whose commission as adjutant was older than Gray's commission at lieutenant. On the same principle his surgeon, who was higher in rank than either, ought to have assumed the command.

Capt. Lloyd has promised me that he will do something for Charley Connely, who is Sergeant Major of the regiment. It seems to me that Charley ought to be entitled to a lieutenancy now, for several officers in the 121st have resigned, among them George Plumer. I intend to see about it soon. The Philadelphia officers seem to have the matter their own way in that regiment, but they all wish to resign, and I presume an opening could be very easily made for Charley before spring by simply procuring the acceptance of the resignation which is most beneficial to him. Charley is all over military, and would make a good captain.

Yesterday we were engaged in making out a list of our officers now present, and of casualties among those who are not with us. The latter was a pretty sad one. We have suffered considerably.

In transmitting the blanks for this report the War Department was guilty of something like a bull. They sent two complete sets of blanks in one package with orders to us to make out two sets of returns and transmit them by different mails to ensure the reception of one set, in the event of the other being lost. Snowden and I concluded, that if such a precaution was necessary with the returns, it was certainly equally necessary with the blanks which the department had sent all in one bundle.

I cannot see much hope of being mustered in as Colonel. I saw Amos Myers and Col. Webster, of Maryland, while in Washington. Webster is now an M. C., and is fully convinced of the injustice done by the order to which I have heretofore referred.

There are three officers in the 1st brigade as now organized who rank me, viz.: Roy Stone, Col. Wister and Col. Dana. Wister is trying to resign. Stone is at Washington, lame from a wound received at Gettysburg. I think he will be made a brigadier. I should like to have my muster as Colonel, for then I would stand a fair chance of being in actual command of the brigade before a year. It is some advantage in the way of comfort to be in that position, besides being highly respectable in the event of being killed. It ensures a fellow a decent funeral.

Camp at Culpeper C. H., Va.,
Jan. 30, 1864.

My Dear Brother:

The weather until this morning and for a whole week has been beautiful. It was so warm that men sought the shady sides of their cabins for loafing places. During this period of sunshine amusements became the order of the day. On Wednesday I dedicated a cabin which the men had built for me. The entertainment consisted of peach toddy, made out of fresh (can) peaches, sugar, nutmeg and commissary whisky. It is a very pleasant drink, and a decided improvement on apple toddy. About a dozen officers favored me with their presence. The staff from division headquarters, an agreeable and intelligent set of young men, came in a body. Among the rest were two field officers of the One Hundred and Forty-third—Colonel Dana and Major Conyngham. The latter is a son of Judge Conyngham, of Luzerne county. He is a fine looking young man, well educated and a lawyer by profession. Colonel Dana served as a captain in the Mexican War. He is a good lawyer and a fine scholar. He is beside, a very accomplished and finished gentleman.

It is some consolation to me in the trials and chances

of the service to know that many better men than myself are suffering the same inconveniences and privations. Then the society of such men is very agreeable. A talk with Dana will dispel the blues at any time.

Talking about privations and hardships, the history of yesterday, for instance, might convey an impression that the army is not the most miserable body of men after all. It was a lovely day, and the scenery around us was beautiful. A review of the First Division came off at 2 o'clock. I rode over with Colonel Dana. The display was very fine, although the division is much reduced, but it has a fine New York brass band in it, and the One Hundred and Forty-first, Brooklyn regiment, with their red pants, is alone worth riding some miles to see. A number of ladies were present. At the close of the review we went by invitation over to the headquarters of General Rice at a large farm house, and partook of some refreshments, to-wit, a glass of very poor whisky. Still the ride was very pleasant. We returned with General Kenley and staff. Coming through Culpeper at corps headquarters I was hailed by Mr. Hays. The General, Aleck, was there, too, and Miss Rachel McFadden, whom you know, was mounted on a lively little horse. She was laughing just as heartily as ever. Aleck rode a fine black horse, and he went through the street just as he used to at Franklin when Lydia was with him. On the whole the meeting was calculated to make one feel younger. I forgot all about the General and his staff, and remained with Aleck's people until they dashed out of town like a party of guerillas. Aleck commands a division of the Second Corps, now lying at Steremburg. They invited me to attend church there to-morrow.

In the evening, yesterday, a small party of us visited a gentleman in town for the purpose of hearing some music. We have a private in our regiment who sings well, and performs on the piano. He used to be a member of the Continental vocalists. His name is Hall, and he is called "Professor." He was one of the party. He played and sang all his songs. A Virginia gentleman played the flute. Captain Cowdrey, of division staff, and myself played chess. We had no other entertainment. One of Hall's songs, "E Pluribus Unum," was received with great favor. The lady of the house informed us that the words were by Mrs. Pendleton, a cousin of her's. We left about 10 o'clock.

The paymaster will not visit us until after the first of March. The government is now behind time in paying troops. The veterans are taking all the money. I will find it very inconvenient to wait another month for my allowance, but this is one of the necessary annoyances of the service.

Lieutenant Colonel Huidekooper, of the One Hundred and Fiftieth Regiment, called a few minutes ago. He lost an arm at Gettysburg. He is from Meadville.

Shannon is in his regiment (Wister's). Huidekooper complains of Governor Curtin's treatment. It seemed strange to me that the Governor should have been rude to an officer who was crippled in the service, for he is a gentleman. Perhaps there may be another side to the story.

This day is cold and damp. I presume we will soon have some more winter.

Camp at Culpeper C. H., Va.,
Monday, Feb. 8, 1864.

My Dear Brother:

We have had pretty exciting times since Friday, another mud march, and, so far as this corps is concerned, nobody hurt, but I am afraid the loss of life in other parts of the army has more than overbalanced the advantages gained by the move.

I was down in Culpeper at a negro minstrel entertainment on Friday evening. Nearly half the officers of our division were there. The affair had been got up by the Brooklyn regiment. It displayed considerable talent. A boy sang a McClellan song. It was loudly applauded. Another minstrel added a verse somewhat detrimental to little Mac's reputation, and it was also cheered, but not quite so vigorously. There are some officers in the army pretty bitter against McClellan. The general feeling, however, is in his favor.

About 10 o'clock, during the performance, a telegram was received by General Newton, who was present. It soon got noised about that it contained marching orders, but I could not learn that it was reliable until after I reached my quarters, when an order came to be ready to move at 3 o'clock in the morning with three days' rations in haversack. The move did not commence, however, till 7 in the morning. We marched down toward the river. Cannonading soon commenced on the left toward Morton's Ford. It began to look serious. When about a mile and a half from the river our division was formed in line in the woods, and there we lay until yesterday evening, when we marched back again.

All day Saturday the cannonading continued at intervals. In the evening there was sharp musketry all down about Morton's Ford, and near enough to sound unpleasantly. It commenced raining Saturday noon and continued all night. I had taken a fly with me, and a good supply of provisions. Will Stehley rendered good service by returning to camp and bringing us out supplies and newspapers. The fly protected us from the rain, and we were not at all uncomfortable physically, but the prospect of having to cross the river was not very agreeable. We were spared that part of the arrangement. On Sunday, yesterday, we lay in the same place. There was some cannonading on our right and left. We heard that part of the Second Corps had crossed the river on Saturday at Morton's Ford, and been driven back with a loss of two hundred men. It became clear again yesterday afternoon, and we received orders at sundown to fall in and march back to camp. The roads in the meantime had become very bad. It was starlight, but the men were often nearly mired in bad places. We reached camp about 9 o'clock, very glad that the move was over.

It was rumored that the object of the move was to attract the enemy's attention and prevent Lee sending re-inforcements to other points. It is now reported that

he is threatening a flank movement by way of Sperry-
ville, and that his infantry is at Madison Court House.
Unless the mud should dry up very rapidly it will not be
easy, however, for any heavy operations to be carried
on this month.

Yesterday while reposing under my fly and wondering
what would come next, I received two very long and interesting letters from you, and another from my wife.
One of yours contained two newspaper extracts. That
charge of the Light Brigade was very well described,
but it seems there were some left to tell the tale. After
reading Tennyson's verses I thought they were all killed.

I presume the extract giving Booth's opinion of Mc-
Clellan is not true, but even if it is true, it proves nothing. I have never yet seen the residence of that distinguished Virginian nor himself. Should I ever meet him
I may inquire whether the paper contains his sentiments.
I presume McClellan will be the Democratic candidate.
The party should not make a nomination too early. In
times like these a month may make a total revolution in
popular sentiment. If the Democrats nominate early,
and put Mac on the track, the Republicans might be compelled to take Grant. On the other hand, if the Republicans nominate first, Lincoln will probably have the best
chance for the nomination. I believe, with McClellan,
that we can beat either Lincoln or Chase. Grant, too, is
probably more popular now than he ever will be again.
I doubt whether either he or any other man can bring
the war to a successful conclusion this year on the Radical platform.

I have heard nothing more about promotion since I
wrote last. I guess the report from Washington did not
amount to much. I shall wait awhile and see what prospect there is, and if I cannot be mustered in as Colonel I
will resign. The more I think of the order which abol-
ishes the office in every regiment which is reduced below
the minimum by losses in battle the more unreasonable
and unjust it appears. I do not allow myself to think
of it much, for it makes me feel discontented.

I must close soon, for the mail is about leaving. I am
still in good health.

BATTLE FLAGS 142D PENNSYLNANIA VOLUNTEERS,
From a photo taken by the permission of Adjt.-Gen. Thomas Stewart.

Camp at *Culpeper C. H., Va.,*
Saturday, Feb. 13, 1864.

My Dear Brother:

Since I wrote last I have received from you, I believe,
two letters and a Harper's Magazine. Your last refers
to the matter of promotion. I have heard nothing more
on the subject since my last, and my mind is quite at
ease about it. It was reported that Colonel Roy Stone
had been appointed. He commands the brigade when
he is here, but that seldom happens. Should he receive
a star he will gain it by virtue of a very small amount of
service in the field. Still he has pretty good reason to
expect it, for his name was once sent to the Senate at a
time when the President nominated a very large number
of Brigadiers, more than the law warranted. It is said,
however, to-day that Stone has not been appointed. He
was wounded at Gettysburg, and has been in Washington ever since, able to walk about and work for promotion, but not able to go to the front. My chance of being mustered in as Colonel is improving. They are sending down some recruits to the army. I am going to
make an effort to have my regiment filled up.

Things here have resumed the same quiet appearance
as before the last move, but you are aware that these
seasons of repose are often suddenly interrupted. Women are still permitted to visit the army. Many officers
have their wives here. Theatrical entertainments on the
parlor or private order are much in vogue. I have two
invitations for this evening, but have concluded not to
go. The Fourteenth Brooklyn has a considerable
amount of musical and dramatic talent in it. The negro
minstrel performances of that regiment in Culpeper are
quite amusing. The last evening "Banjo" addressed
"Bones," and told him of a little ride that he had taken
with General Newton to see a girl. She was a fast woman. Her name was Rapid Ann. They got down near
where she was and found so many fellows cuttin' round
her that they concluded to put off the visit. As the
General himself was present, the joke passed off very
pleasantly.

There was a review to-day near our camp, of Merritt's

6

Division of Cavalry.   The column passed twice before
the reviewing officer.   The bands played pretty well.
When the column passed the second time at a trot, it
was really exciting.   There were about twenty ladies
present at the review, nearly all wives of officers.

One of the assistant surgeons has his wife in Culpeper.
They are from Philadelphia.   She is a real rollicking,
cheerful, mischievous creature, and some of her oddi-
ties excite considerable suspicion.   She is, however, perhaps as good as other people—not quite as good as
Caesar's wife.   She visited me the other day in company with the doctor, and took dinner with us.   Will
Stehley had just received a box from home, and he was
kind enough to give her some confectionery and fruit
cake.   The favor seemed to be highly appreciated, for
such articles are rare in this locality.

We have received no pay for three months.   Yesterday we got a new commissary at brigade headquarters.
He refuses to sell officers their supplies on credit.   The
army regulations require cash, but the same regulations
require the troops to be paid every two months.   Many
of our officers have no money at all.   We have hopes,
however, that the paymaster will arrive in a week or
two.

The weather is still fine, just like spring.   The roads
are drying up very fast.   Our camps look very clean and
tidy.   On all points we are much better off than we were
last winter.   The country around Culpeper is beautiful,
even at this season.   It is much like the Cumberland
Valley, for the Blue Ridge chain is a very striking feature in the landscape, and it is fifteen or twenty miles
distant.   A large stream of water would make this one
of the most romantic spots in the world.

We have again got a fiddle in camp and some of our
men are playing it nearly all the evening.   Others sing
Methodist hymns, and to hear the sounds this moonlight
evening one would hardly suppose that we were in the
midst of a war, and so far in front as to need but a
march of two hours to meet the enemy.

George Snowden has just dropped into my cabin.   He
thinks of resigning.   His experience in the army will be

of great use to him. George has kept a diary regularly
ever since he came out. It will be a pretty good historical document.

Camp near Culpeper C. H., Va.,
Feb. 29, 1864.

My Dear Brother:

The paymaster arrived on Friday and paid us up to
the 21st of December. We have mustered to-day for
two months more, but there is no knowing when it will
suit the powers to settle.

The Sixth Corps went out toward Madison Court
House on Saturday. We have not heard enough firing
in that direction to indicate that they have yet met with
any opposing force. This corps has been under orders
to be ready to move on short notice.

I am in bad luck just now. The House of Representa-
tives passed an amendment to the Senate enrollment bill
which, if it had been concurred in, would have enabled
me to be mustered in as Colonel, but the Committee of
Conference struck it out. This settles my prospect of
promotion for the present. If I could be mustered I
would stand third in rank in the regimental commanders
of the brigade, and Stone's promotion or resignation,
one or the other of which is very probable, would put me
second in rank. But now there is nothing for it but to
wait till we are filled up, and the prospect of receiving
any recruits is very small.

It is only a few minutes since I learned that the Committee of Conference had struck out the House amendment. It was quite a damper. Besides, this is one of
those cold, damp, cloudy days that make a man look on
the dreary side of everything. I could take up the Book
of Ecclesiastes and appropriate the sentiments of the
preacher from beginning to end.

The fine weather seems to be over. We have had a
remarkable month, only three days very cold, and no
rain or snow of any account. The roads are dry. Re-

views, balls and jollifications have been the regular order of exercises. We must have some weeks of mud and rain and sleet before spring comes in earnest, and I think the bad season is about commencing. It makes me shiver to think of marching and lying out at such a time. And we have good reason to apprehend a movement of some sort, but it will not probably accomplish much.

I had a letter from Cossfroth, M. C., from Somerset county. He is a friend of mine, and is blowing some about making me a Brigadier, but there are half a dozen good reasons why he cannot accomplish anything. Accordingly I shall not look for it.

I was much distressed to hear of John Evans being so ill. Poor aunt has had a sad lot. God keep her. I thought about her yesterday evening nearly half an hour. She has not known anything but trouble for many years. And yet I, with health and prosperity, grieve over a few months delay in a trifling promotion.

Another disappointment occasioned by the movement of the Sixth Corps was my failure to get another leave of absence. My application had gone to corps headquarters regularly approved when the order to have the corps held in readiness for a move, stopped everything in the leave and furlough line.

But even in this disappointment I have some consolation. Traveling is expensive, and if I were on leave I would spend a great deal of money that my wife can apply to better purposes than those for which I would probably use it. There is nothing like philosophy. It is consoling but not exhilarating. It is like the gentle stimulating influence of tobacco. It tranquilizes without intoxicating. It assuages grief without exciting merriment.

Dr. Keely and myself, while sitting in the rain one night by a camp fire, beguiled the time by endeavoring to convert ourselves to the stoical doctrine that pain is imaginary. I have tried the same thing when suffering with the toothache. Religion is, however, I believe, a better remedy for such ills, but the trouble is that few persons have enough of it to serve any practical purpose.

A firm faith in a happy future beyond the grave ought to make its possessor cheerful under the worst calamity. But who has such faith? Who is there who is not more elated by the immediate prospect of a successful money speculation than by the remote hope of eternal life? The rest of this sermon will be postponed.

Washington, D. C., March 18, 1864.

Dear Brother:

I am ordered on recruiting service until April 1st. I will go to Harrisburg to-night and remain there probably two weeks.

Harrisburg, Pa., April 4, 1864.

Dear Brother:

I arrived here yesterday from Pittsburg, and received your letter. I was much pleased with the sale of Pithole. I am satisfied with the matter either way, but I presume $44,000 with stock is better than $50,000 without it.

Colonel Bomford is very kind. It is not yet determined whether I will remain here. The Colonel wishes me to stay a few days.

Harrisburg, Pa., April 9, 1864.

Dear Brother:

I have just received an order from the War Department detailing me for duty as commandant of Camp Curtin. Colonel Bomford did the business. His remembrance of you was probably the main reason for his action.

Allequippa, April 11th,

My Dear Brother:

I received a letter yesterday from Alfred informing me of his appointment as commandant of Camp Curtin. We are not going to Harrisburg for some time. He will get a quiet boarding place before I will venture with the children there. Give my love to Lizzie, and tell her when I get to Harrisburg I expect to hear often of her and her family. I felt very sorry for mother when I heard Alex. Wilson had enlisted, but it is what we must all make up our minds to in these *troublous times*. Pittsburg is very pleasant, all sorts of entertainments, and everybody looking forward to the fair with pleasure. Will you please put the sewing machine on a boat and direct to Uncle McCandless' care. Every machine is in requisition, and I feel as if mine would be an accommodation. The children are all well and enjoying themselves very much. Good-bye. God bless you all.

Yours,

S. F. McCalmont.

Harrisburg, Pa., May 9.

Dear Brother:

The army news is very encouraging. You have heard all. The fate of Alexander Hays will be as sad news to you as to me. It is no matter about his faults now. One of them was that he did not appreciate his friends. He had his father's failing on that point. But he is gone, poor fellow. I will always remember him with warm feelings. He had many generous impulses. The poor old man, his father, is now nearly childless. It seems hard for a man to outlive his line.

I again request that you will not do anything toward putting my name forward for Congress. The extremists of our party have gotten us into such a position that there is no prospect of success, and I cannot endure the present administration. I do not say much about politics here. There never is much propriety in political discussions and wrangles.

Harrisburg, Pa., May 13, 1864.

My Dear Brother:

I am still here without any intimation of orders to leave, though it is possible the camp will be vacated ere long. It seems to be diminishing in importance.

I have almost held my breath at the news from the army, but it seems to be clearing up. I could not make a victory out of the first two or three days' operations, but the fact that the Rebels fell back, and that in the last fight they lost about thirty pieces of cannon, seems to leave no doubt about our success. One almost shudders to think how near a defeat it must have been. Our army should have been stronger. We should have run no risks. Fifty thousand more troops would have saved us twenty thousand men.

I have heard little news save what you have read in the papers. Major Warren, commanding my regiment, behaved well. Several officers in it were wounded. One fine young man from Fayette county, Lieutenant Collins, was shot through the heart. He was commanding Company H.

Colonel Dana, One Hundred and Forty-third, was wounded and taken prisoner. I have written about him before in my letters to you. He was a lawyer of some prominence from Luzerne county, and a friend of Judge Woodward. His Lieutenant Colonel (Musser) was killed. The field officers in our brigade must have suffered severely, for I understand our Major (Warren) now commands it. Since I have heard from him, however, he may be killed also. The losses in officers seem to have been terrible. I have seen Hoover Shannon's name in the list of wounded, but have no other information about him.

I am satisfied that I escaped the terrible trial. It is

true it would have been more creditable to have been with my men, but when I sat down to tea this evening with my wife and children I had no regret for the lost honor. Probably I will have still ample opportunity to be in as many fights as will be at all agreeable. The facilities for dying for the country are numerous.

The end is not yet, though things look more hopeful. With every success the powers demand new and more rigorous terms. Will they not learn the policy of being moderate in the hour of victory?

Tell mother that just now there is not much to be done for Aleck, but I trust the result of the victory will be to lighten the work of the western troops, and, may God grant it, to close the war. It seems as if all the good men were to be sacrificed.

It has been raining here for two days. It is probable that the same kind of weather prevails on the Rappahannock, and it may delay operations.

Love to mother and your family. I feel grateful to-night that I have been spared a share in this last struggle. As you once well remarked, a man must recognize other claims as well as those of his country, and I am satisfied that I would have been justified in resigning six months ago. I have no idea of resigning now, however, and if ordered to my regiment, I shall go without murmuring.

Harrisburg, May 14, 1864.

Dear Brother:

My wife and children are well. I have no intimation of being sent to the front, but the Telegraph (Republican) is abusing Bomford every day, and perhaps he will be removed. I have escaped some hard fighting, and can go now with cheerfulness wherever ordered.

Harrisburg, Pa., May 16, 1864.

Dear Brother:

I have still no intimation of any change in my orders. It is true, just now, I am of no use here, but my regiment is not now larger than a full company, and I cannot see that I would be of any more service in front. I shall not make any effort either to remain or to be ordered to the front, but shall obey orders. It would not do to resign just now.

The war news is encouraging, but the thing is not over. I learn from a gentleman just from Washington that re-inforcements are going forward to Grant every day.

My regiment has suffered considerably. I have not heard full particulars. Another captain has been killed in it.

I had a talk with old ex-Governor Porter. He evidently inclines to the idea that the Democrats ought to go for Grant.

I presume McClellan cannot be elected now. The question is how to get an administration that will sink the nigger and go in for a practical restoration of the Union. I believe a General is better than a civilian just now, because the men who are engaged in war know and feel how great a curse it is, and want it ended.

Any change almost would be for the better. On the subjugation platform we will never have peace at all.

Harrisburg, Pa., May 23, 1864.

Dear Brother:

I have seen several persons from the army lately. The Eighth Pennsylvania Reserves passed through town on their way to Pittsburg. Officers of that regiment tell me that Grant has received re-inforcements since the fight, to an extent sufficient to overbalance his losses. Some estimate the re-inforcements at 70,000. They have sent off every available man from Washington. The heavy artillery regiments have been sent to the front.

They say Grant beats McClellan digging. The men are constantly using the spade.

There is no mistake about our army having achieved a victory, but the loss is heavy and the position of the enemy still very strong. More fighting was expected every day.

They say the troops are kept on the move a great deal. There is more manoeuvering than formerly. The Reserve officers say that Meade appears to be the manager, in fact.

Our regiment lost 138 men in killed, wounded and missing—about half of the number present for duty.

The Reserves did not fight as well as formerly. The near approach of the end of their term, and the refusal to allow them to be mustered out will account for this.

Major Over will be under charges again. One officer told me that nothing can save him this time. I am sorry for it, for Over was always very friendly toward me, and he is an admirable drill officer.

Harrisburg, Pa., June 6, 1864.

My Dear Brother:

This has been a great day here in consequence of the return of the Pennsylvania Reserves. Not having any part in the ceremonies, I found a cool place on the balcony of the Jones House and sat there patiently an hour or more while the procession was forming. At last the firing of cannon announced that it was moving. First the escort came down Market street. It consisted of the battery of artillery stationed here. Then came the Reserves, looking very sunburnt, and miserably reduced in numbers. One regiment, the Seventh, had only about twenty men in it. I kept a sharp lookout for the Tenth. Captain Phipps was at the head of it on foot. I went down and spoke to him, and would have walked along with him, but just then some person brought him a horse, and he finished the business up in due form.

The procession was not long in passing. The main civic feature of it was the fire engines. One of them had steam up, and the whistle of the blamed thing blew till everybody was nearly deaf. I do not know whether the steam was exhausted or whether the thing was suppressed as a nuisance, but at any rate, when the procession came back again the noise was stopped. They moved down Market street to the bridge, then down Front street, then over to Second, up Second to State street, and then up State street to the capitol.

There was great enthusiasm manifested by the people. There was great waving of handkerchiefs and immense cheering. When they passed the square the second time every soldier had a bouquet of flowers stuck in the end of his musket, and the officers were still more abundantly supplied. On the whole it was a very fine demonstration, and somewhat touching in its suggestions. It was not easy to witness it with dry eyes.

At the capitol speeches were made, but nobody heard much of them. I stood within ten feet of the speakers, and only made out a few sentences. But the men cheered intensely, and I presume the remarks were eloquent. The Governor and other speakers were shaded, while addressing the audience, by a green umbrella, a point which a historical painter would be very apt to overlook fifty years hence. The speeches were delivered from the steps of the Executive Building or Auditor General's office.

After all was over the Reserves came out to camp. I have seen a good many of the officers this afternoon, and heard a great deal of the recent movements. They estimate Grant's force variously, but the most reliable of them put it at about 150,000.

It seems the Reserves ran like good fellows in the fight a week ago, but they rallied and gave the Rebels a complete dressing. The latter, seeing their temporary confusion, advanced very confidently and were in turn driven back with great loss. From all I can learn the advance was very hazardous, and if the men had not fallen back would have lost the whole division.

I have heard a great many kind remarks made about you by your old soldiers. I never heard anything else among them.

They all have a very high opinion of General Meade, but think that Grant has more pertinacity. Spades are in demand again. An order came yesterday for all the picks and shovels that could be furnished, and several thousand were forwarded. I presume the taking of Richmond is going to be a work of some time.

I have been writing this merely to put in the time before going to bed.

Harrisburg, Pa., June 13, 1864.

Dear Brother:

The Reserves are still here, but some of them will succeed in getting mustered out to-day. They had great difficulty in making out their rolls.

There are eight more regiments of Pennsylvania Volunteers to be discharged this month, and five or six in July. My camp will therefore probably not be broken up, and I may remain here a month longer.

I heard from the regiment the other day. It has not been in any more hard fights since the Wilderness. The division is lying within fourteen miles of Richmond.

The prospect of taking the city immediately is not very bright. It is not easy to see that Grant is any nearer that result than McClellan was at the corresponding date in the year 1862.

As soon as the $300 exemption is repealed there will be another draft. I expect it will be a pretty heavy one, and it will come harder on the people than any of the past ones. I think the money commutation is all wrong, but the draft ought to have been made last winter. The men will not reach the field in time for service in this campaign, and we may be defeated in the meantime for want of them.

Should Grant succeed in spite of the miserable management at Washington, he will indeed deserve credit. He has been much more favored than ever McClellan was, but still the administration has not even yet come up to the demands of the time.

Harrisburg, Pa., July 20, 1864.

Dear Brother:

I have had enough to do during the last few days. I have hardly had time to eat. We have about two thousand one hundred days' men in camp and they are still arriving. So far I have got along without much complaint from any quarter, except the women, whom I have excluded. It was found that under pretense of selling pies and doing washing, they stole large quantities of blankets, tents and other property, and that they carried on prostitution to an extent that would seem incredible. They used to come up in droves. Now we are not favored by them.

The Harrisburg Telegraph is severe on Colonel Bomford. It all arises out of his refusal to give the editor his printing. Bomford will perhaps be relieved.

I have not been in town often for a week. The last time was on Monday evening for a few hours. There was quite a gay company at the Jones House. Generals Sigel and Couch were there. The former played the piano. Some lady sang like a regular prima donna.

I have seen General Couch frequently lately. He is a very agreeable man. Mrs. Couch is a very modest, unpretending lady, and is very generally esteemed. My wife is delighted with her.

General Sigel gave Bob a glass of wine. The young rascal thought it was a grand honor.

After a long dry spell, with any amount of dust, we

have at last had a shower of rain. This evening is cool
and pleasant. The promise of a comfortable sleep is
quite refreshing. At night Oliver and I have the building to ourselves, but business commences at daylight and
then there is nothing but a rush till after dark.

Harrisburg, Pa., July 23, 1864.

My Dear Brother:

Colonel Bomford has been relieved under the pressure
of the attacks in the Harrisburg Telegraph. I cannot
find that my own appointment here, or anything that I
have said or done has been laid against him as objection-
able. I have not been alluded to in any manner.

It is somewhat singular that I have escaped, for there
has been any amount of complaining about almost everybody.

General Irwin has been appointed Adjutant General
during the temporary abdication of Aleck Rupell. Aleck,
they say, has unfortunately been on a big drunk and has
used pretty rough language about the President and
others in authority. But this is confidential. Rupell has
been very kind to me personally.

We have twenty companies of one hundred men in
camp. They are to be sent to Washington to-morrow
evening. I am sitting up late to sign requisitions when-
ever wanted. I have been very busy for a week. They
do not give me time to eat. I have only seen my wife
twice, I think, since last Sunday.

Harrisburg, Pa., Aug. 25, 1864.

My Dear Brother:

The Fifth Corps has been in a big fight. I presume
my regiment was engaged, but I have heard nothing
definite. Colonel Durhane, of the Seventh Maryland,

was killed. I was well acquainted with him. The corps, it seems, held its position on the railroad after a stubborn contest. If it is able to maintain itself there, the point will be a considerable gain.

I think now if we are not compelled to raise the siege of Richmond this fall it will be nearly as much as we can expect. It is not very probable that it will be taken. The demonstration in the Shenandoah looks threatening again. The Rebels there are apparently too strong for Sheridan. There are still two months for active operations, and a strong probability of them closing in Virginia without a decisive result.

I think the election will go against the administration. The President is not popular. He is despised, I believe, or held in very slight esteem by his own party and nearly everybody else. Nothing can save him, but the idea that his election is necessary to prevent the South from dictating their own terms. With McClellan for a candidate there would be no such apprehension. If an unconditional peace man is nominated at Chicago we will be defeated.

I do not talk politics. Judge Scofield, as a sort of fishing interrogatory, said to me the other day: "Who is going to be nominated by your party at Chicago, or is it still your party?" Without apparently noticing the last part of the question, I replied "McClellan." We did not have any discussion about it. I think Scofield is not a very great admirer of the Rail Splitter.

Harrisburg, Pa., Aug. 31, 1864.

My Dear Brother:

I have a great deal of work just now. There are about three thousand men in camp. One regiment has gone, and three more will be organized this week. Some of the officers wish me to take the Colonelcy of one of them, but I am not quite satisfied to do it. It is the only way I can get promotion, but I do not know that it would be in other respects of any advantage. I would be in a brigade commanded by some man who has seen less service than myself, which was one of the evils incident to the life in Virginia.   Then the idea of leaving my wife and children in a week for another winter campaign is not agreeable.   I think I shall decline the proffered honor.   The term of service would be precisely the same, however, as that which is left to me now in my own regiment, but I would have no excuse for resigning, and it may be necessary for me to leave the army soon.

All the newspaper intelligence to-day is cheering.   I am delighted by the nomination of McClellan.   If some great and decisive result is not attained by our armies in a month he will be elected, which will be a glorious event. If some great and decisive result should be attained we can afford to see him defeated, but I cannot see hope of such a change in military operations and fortunes as to reverse the tide of public sentiment which appears to be setting in very strongly against the Rail Splitter.

My boy Oliver has left me and enlisted.   I believe he got about five hundred dollars.   He might have got a thousand as a substitute, but he would not wait a day or two at my suggestion.

Bounties seem to have gone mad.   Each regiment gets · about a half a million of dollars.   It is all paid in new bank notes of county banks.   The increase of paper circulation in this month will be fearful, probably twenty millions of dollars.   We cannot carry on a war very long at this rate.   We must come down to the Southern system or quit.   Still the South is much worse off, and I believe, very anxious for peace.   The election of McClellan may change the tone of public sentiment in that region.

COL. A. B. McCALMONT,
Before Petersburg, Va., 1865.

Harrisburg, Pa., Sept. 11, 1864.

My Dear Brother:

I have accepted the appointment of Colonel in the Two Hundred and Eighth Regiment, and will leave Harrisburg soon.

It seems my decision was pretty fortunate. The War Department issued an order on the 7th appointing Colonel Roy Stone to this post. I think it would have been all the same whether I had taken a regiment or not.

The War Department has telegraphed that my transfer and promotion are all right. I presume I will be mustered to-day. I will have a fine, large regiment.

Harrisburg, Pa., Sept. 21, 1864.

Dear Brother:

The news from Sheridan is cheering. I would have no objection to a victory by Grant before going to the front.

Harrisburg, Pa., Oct. 10, 1864.

My Dear Brother:

Captain Dodge, commanding the post, reports to the War Department that I have done "a vast amount of work" and done it "well." He also reports that I can join my regiment without *detriment* to the service (quite a compliment), but that if I go immediately the rolls will have to be forwarded to me in the field for signature. So I will probably either stay to sign them or come back to do it, for they will hardly send me three hundred rolls by mail to be signed.

7

Harrisburg, Pa., Oct. 18, 1864.

My Dear Brother:

I have not yet received my order to join my regiment, but my work is nearly finished and I will go as soon as it is done.

I have had intimations from several sources that if I were to change my political views and make a few stump speeches on the other side it would be greatly to my advantage. I shall not avail myself of these offers or any of them. I have done so many things wrong in my life that I cannot afford to carry with me the consciousness of having been actually sold.

Harrisburg, Pa., Nov. 4, 1864.

My Dear Brother:

I have been detained here much longer than I expected. I am now, however, ready to go, and will leave certainly on Monday. I could have, by hurrying, gone to-day, but the old superstition about Friday made me dilatory.

I sent you my proxy. After it had gone I had a dim suspicion or recollection that Squire Klein had omitted to sign the authority as a witness. I hope, however, that it will prove to be all right. My position here as a McClellan man is well known. I have not been very talkative, but have not courted favor by pretending to be on the other side. A Republican correspondent volunteered to give me a puff in a Philadelphia paper. Then he read it to me, and then he wanted to borrow ten dollars. By the way, there is a great deal of borrowing here. I am out of pocket considerably on that score, though the most of my creditors of that kind have paid me.

I presume McClellan will be defeated, but it cannot be helped. He will make a pretty strong run under the circumstances. This will have some effect in controlling the action of the administration. I saw William H. Miller this morning. He was candidate for Congress here,

and is a member of the old Congress. He has recently
seen McClellan, and has a high opinion of his abilities.

Rather a good thing has happened lately as an illustration of the beauties of the detective system. The government employed five or six men to come here a month
ago when the new regiments were being formed, for the
purpose of keeping a watch on the officers, and prevent-
ing bounty jumping. Merely to show how the thing
could be done (?) they enlisted under fictitious names.
Each man enlisted and was mustered in this way four or
five times, each time drawing five hundred dollars local
bounty. Of course, the purpose was to illustrate the facil-
ity by which the fraud could be perpetrated, but when
the matter came to be sifted, it turned out that the de-
tectives had vamosed and taken all the money with them.
The elephant, that was taught to put a dime on the top
of a post out of reach, but was not taught how to get it
down again, affords a fair illustration of this nice little
swindle. I have precious little confidence in the detective
system, or the Jesuitical policy of using fraud to defeat
fraud. It makes more rascals than it punishes.

I feel very cheerful about leaving. It is true I had
some regrets at giving up good dinners and a snug bed
to resume camp life, but I have been pretty fortunate
this summer and ought to consider myself as one of the
favored few. I have no particular forebodings about
the consequences, and will do my duty without complaining. I will be in a vein for corresponding after regain-
ing the army and will give you news from time to time.

Saturday, Nov. 19, 1864.
Camp, near Bermuda Landing,
Headquarters 208th Reg. P. V.

My Dear Wife:

I have just received your letter of the 16th. I will
need all the consolation that your dear correspondence
can afford, for this is a dismal place in bad weather. It
has been raining all night, and the storm still continues.

Yesterday afternoon I rode with Lieutenant Colonel

Heintzelman along the line of breastworks. At every point the men were placed on the extreme front, as if anticipating an attack. The subject of conversation everywhere was the capture by the Confederates of Colonel Kauffman, of the Two Hundred and Ninth. We understood that an effort would be made to recapture some of the ground on the picket line, which had been lost the night before. Well, about 9 o'clock last night the musketry fire opened in earnest and continued for about an hour. It was quite dark and there was a cold rain falling. The men who were not on picket were all deployed on the breastwork. I could not see that I had anything to do but remain in one place, for my men were scattered along the line for about a mile. I, however, rode out a short distance toward the right, and shivered a half hour in the rain until the firing ceased. Then I came back with the Lieutenant Colonel and slept soundly until morning. I have not heard what the result was.

The picket line is about one-half mile in front of the breastwork. It extends from the James river on the right, to the Appomattox on the left. Our regiment is on the extreme left of the breastwork and in sight of the Appomattox. The worst part of the duty here is picketing. My turn as general officer of the line will come about once a week. I presume my first experience will be to-morrow. The line runs through a dense pine forest cut up with deep ravines, and it is impossible to ride the entire length of it. The Rebel line is almost within speaking distance of ours.

Our men are in comfortable quarters. They have nice little log cabins. The Lieutenant Colonel and I have a cabin together. It is better than the one I occupied last winter. The fare, too, seems to be good. Indeed, on all points the locality is better than I expected, but still not quite as comfortable as the Jones House.

Tell Mrs. Fenn that Captain Dalien holds daily intercourse with the Rebels. He gave me some Richmond papers yesterday procured in exchange for ours. He has also supplied the cabin with tobacco from the same source. They say that one day he procured some tobacco, and on his way home had the luck to kill a musk-rat. He skinned the animal, and put the skin in the same pocket with the tobacco. Nevertheless the latter is very good. Some think it improves the flavor.

We are in no danger here of forgetting that there is a state of war actually existing. The Rebels fire a shell at Butler's canal about every ten minutes. Then up at Petersburg, some six or eight miles off, they have some kind of Fourth of July entertainment at almost any hour. I have not been here long, but I have already become so much accustomed to the thing that I can distinguish the different shots without difficulty, and hear them without annoyance. The musketry firing, however, on the picket line is unpleasant, when it happens, but it never lasts long at a time.

On the whole I am by no means miserable. This is one of the most dismal days imaginable. The cold storm of wind and rain keeps driving on, and the cannon keep slowly pounding away with a strange sort of dignified pertinacity. There is not much in the situation or circumstances to make life agreeable, and yet I am quite cheerful, have a good appetite and good spirits. I believe the most gloomy feeling I experience is when I look at the poor men on duty in the rain, and what I feel for them by way of sympathy diminishes my own consciousness of personal sufferings. If these poor fellows can stand their lot, I certainly should bear mine.

Headquarters 208th, P. V., 18th Army Corps,
Bermuda Hundred, Nov. 19, 1864.
Dear Brother:

I wrote to my wife this morning and requested her to send the letter to you. I thought it was probable, from the appearance of things, that I would not have an opportunity of writing to-day. I am expecting to be sent out on picket as general officer of the line.

We are lying on the left of a line of breastworks which extends from the Appomattox to the James river. Most of the other one-year regiments, which were organized in September at Camp Curtin, are lying near the same works on our right. The Confederate line of works is about a mile from us, and the picket lines are very near each other. The ground to the front and rear is covered with pine woods, and broken up by deep ravines. Immediately in front of the breastworks there is a slashing, or Jefferson county clearing, somewhat difficult of access.

I came here yesterday and was warmly received. The band, a very good one, gave me a serenade in the evening. About an hour later there was a change of program and a general fire of musketry on the picket line. I began to think I was in for it the first night, but the thing subsided gradually, and I had a comfortable night's sleep.

The regiment is scattered over an extent of a mile, but the companies are still under the same command. They are all in good quarters. All the men have good cabins. Lieutenant Colonel Heintzelman and myself occupy a very comfortable little home, and if we are allowed to spend the winter in it I will not complain, but the present motions indicate rough work. The Confederates night before last made a raid on our picket line and captured the general officer of the day, Colonel Kauffman, of the Two Hundred and Ninth P. V. I understood the fight last night was to re-occupy the ground lost on the evening previous.

It has been raining all night and all day. The weather is very disagreeable for military operations, and the poor men suffer considerably. They have to picket every other day, and the rest of the time, night and day, they are kept under arms at the breastworks. Our batteries on the right fired all morning. They have discontinued since I commenced writing. Up at Petersburg there is some kind of a fight going on all the time. Last night the musketry in that direction was heavy and very distinctly heard here, though it is six or seven miles distant.

We have a signal station a few rods from camp. It is precisely like an oil derrick, but some forty feet higher.

So you see I cannot avoid the eternal greasy subject even here. I thought I would forget all about it.

I am much more comfortably situated than I expected, but this is a dreary place for the Christmas holidays.

I have a very fine regiment. The men are well behaved, and the company officers are a very competent and faithful set of men. We are under a New Hampshire Colonel named Potter, who commands the Provisional Brigade. They say my men are terrible on eating. Many jokes are cracked about their appetites. A proposition has been made to change the army ration. One man, who eats 37 crackers in 24 hours (10 is the allowance), when told that we were in the *Provisional* Brigade, said he did not believe a word of it.

Camp near Peables House,
Nov. 29, 1864.

My Dear Wife:

We arrived here yesterday. On our way we passed the One Hundred and Forty-second, and I wrote you a note at Colonel Warren's cabin. We are now on the extreme left of the line of the Army of the Potomac, but will go back to-morrow to encamp nearer the right of the line and about five miles from City Point. The move is not very easy to comprehend in all its aspects, but it has this explanation, that the Second and Ninth Corps are mutually exchanging positions. The former is moving over here, and the latter is going to the ground recently occupied by the Second. To us the consequence is simply that we must march over the ground which we traveled yesterday. The difficult thing to see through, however, is why the two corps should change places at all. I cannot understand it, but fortunately for the country it is not important that I should be able to comprehend the various movements. There are rumors that the Ninth Corps is going to leave this army, but our Brigadier General does not intimate anything of the kind.

Our march to this point gave us a fine opportunity of seeing the entire army, and the position which it occupies. We have come round so far that the cannon at Dutch Gap and Petersburg are heard in a northeasterly direction, and have the low, sullen sound of very distant thunder.

On our march I met many old friends. Little Will Connely took me by surprise in the pine woods near the One Hundred and Forty-second. I saw nearly all of the One Hundred and Forty-second, and a great many acquaintances in other regiments. We had to report at General Meade's headquarters, where I met Jno. Craig, Captain Bache, who recruited at Franklin, and several other acquaintances on the General's staff. Will Riddle, Major, was indisposed, but I spoke to him at his tent door.

The weather is fortunately very pleasant. We have had no rain and the nights are not very cold. I hope there will be no change until we are permanently located.

The six regiments—Two Hundredth, Two Hundred and Fifth, Two Hundred and Seventh, Two Hundred and Eighth, Two Hundred and Ninth, Two Hundred and Eleventh—are now provisionally brigaded together, and under command of Brigadier General Hartranft. Both he and Major General Park, the corps commander, impressed me very favorably. We will probably be divided into two brigades, and compose together the Third Division, Ninth Corps.

When we are settled in our new camp I will write to you my impressions. Just now there are poor facilities for writing. Should you write to Franklin soon you may enclose this. I am in good health, but rather dirty.

Camp near Petersburg, Va.
Dec. 1, 1864.

My Dear Brother:

On Sunday the white regiments at the defences of Bermuda Hundred including our own were relieved by a lot of colored troops, and we took up our march with orders to report to General Meade. On Sunday night we encamped on this side of the Appomattox, the next day we moved on and reported to General Williams who assigned us to the Ninth Corps, which then lay on the extreme left of the line. The road was all through pine woods and along the line of the military railroad. Before reaching Meade's headquarters I passed the camp of the One Hundred and Forty-Second, and saw many old friends. Willy Connely, who is detailed as a clerk at some division headquarters, spoke to me on the road, and rather surprised me though I knew he was here somewhere.

We did not remain long on the left of the line. An order was already issued for the Ninth and Second Corps to exchange positions. We marched back yesterday morning, and we are now encamped about a mile or less in the rear of our outer line of works in immediate sight of Petersburg, and about eight miles from City Point. The enemy can throw shell into our camp and even to the railroad in our rear. They are throwing a few today but not precisely in our direction. I saw one explode over a piece of woods to our left since I commenced writing. The picket firing here is a settled institution and goes on all night, apparently about as fast as they have time to load. It seems, however, to do very little harm.

We are still in a sort of provisional brigade, but I believe they are organizing a division, Third, of the Ninth Corps to be composed principally of the regiments which were organized in Pennsylvania last fall. General Hartranft commands us. I am very much pleased with him thus far.

Our camp is in an open field once a large Virginia farm. The old mansion which bears marks of better days is occupied by our general for headquarters. Petersburg lies nearly west, and is about two or three miles distant. There is a fort to our left named for General Alexander Hays of Franklin. Not far from us, and nearly in front of us is the "Crater," or blown up fort that was mined last summer, and in the same neighborhood is a work called Fort Hell. From all I can learn this is a pretty rough locality.

I have not heard from you since I left Franklin. I am in excellent health. The weather is very mild, clear and pleasant. We are putting up quarters with a view of remaining permanently. My cabin will be very comfortable. There is some possibility that I will command a brigade in the new organization, but it depends entirely on the manner of grouping the regiments.

Camp at Avery House, Va., near Petersburg,
Dec. 6, 1864.

My Dear Brother:

I went up to the lookout on the Avery House yesterday. It is about thirty rods from our camp. They have some good glasses, and the view is very wide. I took a peep at Petersburg. We could tell the time of day by the town clock. Then we could see camps of the enemy with men washing, combing their hair, lounging and playing. It seemed strange to think that their business was to kill us and ours to kill them.

Last night there was a fire in Petersburg. All the bells were rung, and quite a bright light sprang up. Our guns did not open on the town. The picket firing has declined within the last two days. It was kept up previously without interruption from dark till daylight.

The Sixth Corps, or at least part of it, has returned to this army. It is by no means improbable that troops will be required in Tennessee. I perceive we have had some more *victories* all the time losing ground there. I do not like the appearance of things in that region, and I

expect a corps will be sent out there from this army.   In
that event it will probably be the Ninth.   I shall not be
sorry.   I am tired of Virginia.

I am in excellent health, out of money and somewhat
lousy, but still very cheerful.   I have few wants.

Camp at Avery House, Va.,
Dec. 14, 1864.

My Dear Brother:

We have had four or five very rough days.   We were
sent out to meet the Fifth Corps, which had gone on an
expedition to destroy the Weldon railroad.   The Third
Division of the Ninth Corps had marching orders on Friday evening, but we only went a mile or two that day,
and lay all night in a cold rain which froze as it fell.   All
of Saturday we remained in the same position, and in the
evening moved down the Jerusalem Plank Road.   We
went out about eighteen miles.   It rained all the time.   I
never experienced so rough a march.   We halted about
four o'clock in the morning at the Nottaway or some
other stream.   I have not examined the map.   Here the
Fifth Corps had arrived on their way back.   They
crossed on pontoons on Sunday.   Our division came back
Sunday night.   The rain had ceased.   It was intensely
cold.   I had to walk five miles to keep warm.   Some
cavalry men set fire to every house on the route.   It
made a wild and terrible scene.   We reached camp after
midnight, but were ordered to move again at daylight on
Monday.   We did not go far and after shivering in the
pine woods until yesterday (Tuesday) evening we were
at last permitted to return to our old quarters.

Friday and Saturday nights were the most trying I
ever experienced.   I stood all night Friday near a poor
fire.   My hat and coat were covered with ice half an inch
thick.   When daylight came I felt as glad as Columbus
when he saw land.

The march on Saturday night was very severe.   The
rain had swollen the small streams, and the poor men had

to wade right through. The wind was cold and bitter. Having lost all sleep the previous night you may suppose it was rough enough.

I hope the winter moves are over. There will be, of course, great blowing over the achievements of the Fifth Corps, but I cannot see that much has been done. The men plundered and burnt, but it is doubtful whether the gain will balance the account of frozen feet and ruined constitutions.

Camp at Avery House, Va.,
Dec. 16, 1864.

My Dear Brother:

We have had quite an exciting afternoon. The enemy opened on us with a battery that we had not previously heard from. They seemed to have a particular design on our camp. Several of their shell fell in its limits. One was buried in the ground about five or six rods from my cabin. It exploded after it struck and the surrounding earth prevented it from doing any harm. It seems strange that none of our men were hurt, for about a dozen shots struck close around us, and the poor fellows stood in the most exposed situations to see what was going on. They were scattered all over the field, having company drill when the thing opened.

Our batteries took the matter in hand and opened with spirit, and there was a heavy cannonading kept up from two o'clock till sundown. It appears to have done very little harm on our side. All is now quiet, but the firing of pickets which is generally kept up without interruption all night long. This state of things has become chronic.

The Third Division of the Ninth Corps was organized yesterday. We are in the First Brigade composed of the Two Hundredth, Two Hundred and Eighth, and Two Hundred and Ninth Regiments, Pennsylvania Volunteers, and commanded by Colonel Diven of the Two Hundredth.

We have an official announcement of another victory

by Thomas, also rumors that Savannah has been captured by Sherman, and that the negro troops have taken the Howlett Battery, a formidable fort, which is on the left of the Confederate defences at Bermuda Hundred. I hope that one and all of these items of good news will prove to be true, but you will know by the papers.

I presume I will be detailed as president of the court-martial in a day or two. It will keep my mind employed.

Lieutenant Colonel Dodd of the Two Hundred and Eleventh will be tried for insulting or striking his colonel. He seems to know me, but I cannot think who he can be unless he is a son of Levi Dodd, of Franklin, and brother of Sam. He is a fine looking man, but he will be in a bad fix if the colonel's charges are sustained. However, I do not know but that a man might as well be dismissed as killed or crippled. I think all of my acquaintances who have left the army, either honorably or dishonorably, have been benefited by the change.

Colonel Diven, who commands our brigade, ranks me by a few days. I am the next in rank in the brigade. Diven was a captain in the Twelfth Reserves. I believe he rose to major, but I was lieutenant colonel long before he was a major. This, however, as you know, does not count. It makes very little difference to me about commanding a brigade for there is no advantage in it to my mind worth mentioning, except the privilege of having better quarters on the march.

The evening has resumed the general semblance of all other evenings in this region. Some men are singing Methodist hymns, members of the band in their quarters are practicing on snatches of music with various kinds of horns. Trains of cars occasionally hurry past a short distance in the rear of our camp, and the pickets keep up their steady monotonous firing. I sometimes about this time walk out alone and meditate for an hour, but like all meditation it ends in nothing very definite in result.

Camp at Avery House, Va.,
Dec. 18, 1864.

My Dear Brother:

There is a cold drizzling rain this morning, and the time within doors drags heavily. I find more amusement or relief in writing letters at such times than in anything else. I have read the New York Herald of the 16th clear through. The luminous decision of Judge Coursin discharging the St. Alban's raiders is as clear as mud.

A salute of one hundred guns was fired this morning by a battery in the rear of our camp in honor of the victory of Thomas at Nashville. I am in hopes that another will soon announce the taking of Savannah. The late successes in different quarters give us much reason to hope that the war will be ended. The Confederacy is evidently getting weaker. During the year just closing the Rebels have had only one or two victories of a small kind to set off against almost a dozen very decided Federal triumphs, and although there has been no great result achieved in this quarter it is plain that Grant's army has been steadily gaining ground all the time. In the spot where we are encamped the ground has been contested by inches. Everywhere you can see lines of Confederate entrenchments from which the enemy were driven back by hard fighting, and many of which have been levelled to make clear space for new operations.

If there is anything wanting in our generals here, it would seem to be a want of engineering ability. I cannot help the conviction that we have not enough large guns on our line, and that even those in position are not kept in active use as constantly as they should be. I believe a hundred large guns pounding at this point steadily would reduce Petersburg in thirty days, but I may be mistaken. There are many things that I do not know.

Camp at Avery House, Va.,
Dec. 21, 1864.

My Dear Brother:

After several days of very clear and mild weather, we have now a steady and pretty heavy rain, which threatens to stop raids and movements generally for some time to come, but in our position, where we can be shelled at a moment's notice, it is not necessary to move to realize that a state of war actually exists. Still there is great inconvenience and sometimes suffering on a march at this season, and we would rather bear the ills we have than fly to others that we know not of. We have not been shelled since I wrote last, and probably in a day or two we will move our camp about fifty rods to a spot less exposed to observation. The Two Hundred and Eleventh Regiment, which is lying on our right, is going to move to a point near the other two regiments of the Second Brigade, and we will, I think, take their vacated quarters. There will be several advantages in the change.

I rode over to army headquarters yesterday. It was a very pleasant afternoon. I met some old acquaintances. The place looks as lively as a small city. I was almost lost among the numerous tents.

The news from all points is still very encouraging. The victory in Tennessee is particularly gratifying, because our army there having been weakened, and also having fallen back a defeat was very probable. Under these circumstances it indicates great strength on our side for Thomas to attack the enemy in a fortified position and carry it by storm. This with the encouraging news from Savannah gives ground to hope that the war may be ended successfully. The Southerners are very brave and self-denying, but they cannot stand everything.

We had strong rumors of the death of Jeff Davis, but at army headquarters yesterday I was informed that there was no truth in them.

An application for a leave of absence from one of the captains came back this morning disapproved on the ground that the exigencies of the service would not permit it just now, but it was significant that the endorsement also stated that "probably in a short time it will be favorably considered."

We have not yet seen a pay master. My men have not received a cent of either pay or bounty from the United States. I have about four hundred dollars coming. It will be probably a month before the officer arrives.

Harrisburg, Jan. 1, 1865.

My Dear Brother:

I received your very kind present this morning, I need not say I am obliged. I trust that next year we may all be together, and some of us better and wiser for our past experience. I hear from Alfred almost every day. He still continues well, and is sanguine about the approaching termination of the war. The children are in good health, and at present are occupied skating.

The next letter I receive from Alfred I will enclose.

S. F. McCALMONT.

Camp at Avery House, Va.,
Jan. 10, 1865.

My Dear Brother:

We have nothing new here except a few camp rumors that our corps is to be sent somewhere under General Burnsides, and that General Butler has been relieved. The latter is probably correct. I shall not regret it, if it should be true, for I regard him as a military humbug. The other is more doubtful, for just now there does not seem to be as much need of troops in other quarters as there is here.

I am still sitting on a court-martial. We have tried several officers of the new regiments. There are no cases from the Two Hundred and Eighth. We have a very fine set of line officers, and the men are very obedient and well behaved.

It has been raining hard all day. There has been

some thunder and lightning with it. This is probably not the case in Venango, though I have observed that our cold weather comes on about the same days with that of New York.

For a day or two there has been very little cannonading. To-day there is none at all. There is a dense fog between us and the Rebel lines. The firing has not yet injured any of my men, though the camp is not protected by works, and though several shells have fallen within it.

Camp at Avery House, Va.,
Jan. 19, 1865.

My Dear Brother:

The news of the capture of Fort Fisher was announced yesterday by a salute of one hundred guns. It is a very important achievement. The cause looks hopeful. Butler's removal is to me a source of satisfaction. He is a confounded old demagogue and humbug.

Your two oleaginous publications, the newspaper and magazine, came to hand. I read them clear through. I think they contained a sufficient dose of oil for a month.

Camp at Avery House, Va.,
Jan. 20, 1865.

My Dear Brother:

I rode over to the One Hundred and Forty-second Regiment to-day after our court adjourned for want of business. Our surgeon, Dr. Asay, who has been discharged honorably for physical disability, accompanied me. We had a very pleasant ride. The distance is about three miles. We called on General Crawford, who is commanding the Fifth Corps in the temporary absence of General Warren. It is only a month since that corps took its present position in the rear of the line, and it is surprising how the country has changed. It was then a dense pine forest. Now it is covered with beautiful camps,

8

regularly laid out. The cabins are all neat and comfortable, and the stables are covered with clap boards. General Crawford received us very cordially, and showed us his new quarters. They exhibit great taste. It seems that every time the men build new quarters they improve on their former ones. Our cabins this winter are better than any we have ever had.

We are having reviews and brigade drills every day or two. There is less firing than there was some days ago.

Jan. 22, 1864.

The weather has become very disagreeable. It has rained steadily about twenty-four hours. The roads are bad enough. All cannonading has ceased, and the picket firing is nearly dispensed with. We are living very comfortably. Colonel Heintzelman got a large box from home filled with good eatables. Many of our officers received similar presents. Last evening I took supper with one of them, a Captain named Dalien. He is a Frenchman, who was educated at the school of St. Cyr, and served several years in the French army. He was in the battles of Majenta and Solferino. His descriptions of those fights are very clear and interesting, but last night he related his experience in recruiting. His imperfect English added to the effect. I laughed till I was sore. It would be impossible to put his experience on paper, but I can give you a faint specimen of a part of it. He opened an office to recruit a company, waited two days, nobody came, third day a Canadian came who could only speak French. He could not go any place else for nobody could understand him. Dalien enlisted him, made out five muster rolls, walked all the way to Camp Curtin to have the man mustered, mustering officer said the papers were wrong, offered to make new ones, charged two dollars. Then says Dalien: "I go down, I sit down on ze block where zey sells ze meat and ze vegetables (Market house), I look at ze two paper, my own and ze one made by ze mustering offisair. I see no difference. I compare zem carefullee. I find zem both ze same. Yes, Colnell, both ze same."

Next he misses his Canadian for three days. He is brought to him by an old officer "with wine marks on his face" as a deserter. He is put in the guard house at Camp Curtin. In a few days the old soldier calls and claims the reward of thirty dollars for the arrest, and Dalien compromises.

After going on with his narration of other incidents equally amusing, I at last asked him what became of the Canadian. His reply was the raciest of all. "The Canadienne, Colnell, vot became of him, you say. Why, Colnell, he in ze guard house at Camp Curtin. I forget him in ze hurry coming away. He remain. He no speak ze English. Nobody in Harrisburg speak ze French. He not be able to explain. Probablee, Colnell, he remain zere till ze close of ze war."

Dalien's is an instance of remarkable perseverance. He succeeded in raising a company after all, now Company C. By the exertions of a Mrs. Fenn in Harrisburg, and some of my own, he has received an appointment as aide on the staff of General Hartranft, and his industry and military training will ensure him further promotion.

Jan. 29, 1865.

This evening we have several rumors, one that General Grant has expressed the opinion that the enemy is about evacuating Richmond. Another one is that the Rebels are going to cross the Appomattox, and attack our right to-night, so we are under orders to be ready to move on short notice.

Camp at Avery House, Va.,
Feb. 1, 1865.

Dear Brother:

Before this reaches you the newspapers will announce the admission of Stevens and Hunter and some other Southern gentlemen as commissioners. They came in last evening at sundown in front of this corps. A carriage with four grey horses was waiting for them. The

Rebels and our men all cheered when they came over. It was quite an animating scene. Colonel Heintzelman and myself followed the carriage, after it passed through our camp, to the railway station where a special train was waiting to carry the party to City Point. I recognized Stevens and Hunter when they got out of the carriage. All men here of all parties wish them God speed, if their mission be peace and union.

We are under orders to be ready to move on short notice. I think we will go to-night. I understand our destination is Newbern. I believe our Division alone is going. We shall probably soon be on the briny deep. I feel rather gratified by the change. We have too much monotony here. I have always had an anxiety to see some other part of the field than Virginia. Perhaps I will get enough of it.

Camp at Avery House, Va.,
Feb. 5, 1865.

Dear Brother:

When I last wrote we were under orders to be ready to move at short notice. There was, however, no move. I had reason to think that our Corps or Division was intended to go South. This morning we are again under orders which indicate a very sudden move in some direction. It will probably be over toward the left of the line.

We have heard that Stephens and the other peace commissioners were met at Fortress Monroe by Secretary Seward, and that they returned yesterday. Arrangements were made here for them to go back at the same point where they entered our lines, but they did not arrive here. I was told that they went back by the river route from City Point.

The weather has been mild and clear for several days. We have been drilling by Brigade and Division. The enemy has not been firing much at this point lately. Last night there was heavy cannonading on our right. It seemed to be a fight between gunboats on the Appomattox and a battery which is on the same river about a mile and a half from Petersburg. From the peculiar condition of the atmosphere the sound was like a young earthquake. Each report was like the explosion of a magazine, but the firing was too deliberate and slow to indicate anything more than the usual bombardment.

One of my men returned on Friday from Harrisburg, where he has been on furlough. He brought with him a live turkey as a present to me from his father. He also carried in his knapsack a complete uniform for the Lieutenant Colonel. He was offered five dollars for the turkey by officers at City Point, and he had kept awake on the boat to watch it. His virtue and pertinacity of purpose had been proof against all temptation and hardship. I told him I would not have done as much for my nearest relative.

The other day, when the flag of truce was sent upon the arrival of the peace commissioners, our men and the Rebels took occasion to cut down a tree which stood between the two lines, and which was very desirable for fire wood. About a dozen from each side participated in the frolic. They cut it down, then cut it up and put it in two piles. The choice of piles was amicably settled, and each party returned to their respective camps having accomplished a small peace mission of a very practical character in less time than would take a diplomatist to introduce the subject.

Camp at Avery House, Va.,
Saturday, Feb. 11, 1865.

My Dear Brother:

You have by this time read about the late move. Our Division of the Ninth Corps had some share in it, though we saw no fighting. We moved on Sunday last and returned yesterday. I thought as we were out that we were going to fight, for there was heavy cannonading away to the left and straight ahead of us in our march, but our position was assigned on the right of the Second Corps, and the enemy made no attack on us, and did not appear on our front at all.

We had no tents with us. It rained on Tuesday, and was afterward very cold. We suffered some from the weather, but we were so near the camps on the left of the old line that we got plenty to eat. It seems as if away out there they were better supplied with provisions than we are. They also have better quarters, but we went clear out beyonds the works on the left into the swamps and wilderness. After the first night my regiment lay on the right of the new line, next to the left of the old.

We heard all about the fighting from men who came back, and I saw the field. My regiment was sent over to Second Corps Headquarters yesterday to report to an engineer officer and build corduroy, but the officer did not come, and I did not go to hunt him. He was to meet us at the Tucker House at a certain hour, but he failed to do so, and I had time to look at the ground. We returned in the evening to the Division, and then to this camp.

The movement was intended, I think, merely to straighten the line and extend it to Hatchers Run or as far as practicable, and I think it has been a great success. I will give you a little rough draft showing the old and new positions, i. e., before and since last Sunday. The line has been extended about three miles, and will undoubtedly be held in its present position, for it is very strong.

Feb. 17, 1865.

Colonel Diven having gone home yesterday on a leave of absence I am in temporary command of the brigade. Yesterday as officer of the day I rode along the line of works and pretended to be doing something, but it is by no means probable that any new movement will be inaugurated as the result of my observations. Soon after I returned the enemy's batteries opened, and kept up a vigorous shelling till after sundown. I do not hear of any person being hurt. Soon after dark a thunder storm passed off toward the South. The thunder was mistaken for cannon until it came nearer. I contended that it was thunder, but I confess that my opinion was more in consequence of the direction of the sound than its character.

This is strange weather. The 14th and 15th were the coldest days of the season. Our ink froze beside the fire place with a low fire in it. Yesterday it rained and this morning the roads would carry a horse where yesterday the mud was knee deep, but such changes are common all over the country.

Colonel Diven will return about the 3rd of March. Leaves are now granted for fifteen days. I think I will apply for one on his return. It was intimated to me to-day at Division Headquarters that I had better apply at that time, inasmuch as there may be a general order forbidding leaves as soon as the time for active operations arrives.

They still keep up this fiction about a season for active operations. I can only remember two consecutive months that we did not move somewhere, and they were August and September, 1863. The roads were perfect and the weather pleasant, but we lay in camp at the Rappahannock all the time.

Washington, D. C.,
March 31, 1865.

Dear Brother:

I called on the Secretary of War to-day. His Adjutant had previously heard my explanation of my detention, and caused an order to be entered extending my leave of absence till the second day of April.

Stanton was very kind. He told me he intended to give me a Brevet Brigadiership, and possibly a full one. I did not introduce the subject. He broached it himself. It will be all right after I join the regiment. The appointment just now would seem a little out of place as I was absent during the last fight, but it will be made in due time.

After he had spoken on this subject, Colonel Webster, of Maryland, now a member of Congress, came in. He affected surprise in Stanton's presence that I had not been

promoted. This fitted the occasion very well. Webster
was a Colonel in the First Corps. He and I went to
school together at Carlisle.

Fitzgerald's House,
April 7, 1865.

My Dear Brother:

I believe I have not written to you since I left Washington. I requested you to keep the matter about my
promotion secret, but I believe it will not be long in becoming public. I had some conversation with General
Hartranft this evening over a camp fire about it. He
would be well satisfied to have me command the brigade
permanently, and will give me a letter to that effect.

Fitzgerald's where I am writing is near the South Side
Railroad two miles west of Blacks and Whites station.
When I came to the station this morning about three
o'clock, I asked one of Colonel Dodd's sentinels if that
was "Blacks and Whites." He thought I referred to the
troops, and said "No" and that the colored troops had
gone on ahead. Maybe you think I made this poor joke,
but it is a fact, and being the only pleasant incident of last
night's travel, I have thought it worth mentioning. We
soon found that the sentinel was right, for on coming
through a dark wood our column was halted by a soli-
tary negro posted on the side of the road. He seemed to
be frightened, and being too black to be distinguished
from the darkness around him, his unexpected "halt"
made me a little nervous. Nobody had any right to put
a sentinel on the road, and the pickets whom we were to
relieve having been prematurely withdrawn the possibility
of the fellow being an enemy was by no means too remote
to be despised. I halted, of course, and sent a man to
ascertain the nature of the interruption. This little incident caused some merriment. The idea of one darky
halting our brag brigade is considered a big joke.

Blundering around in the dark for a camping place about
4 o'clock (and I am now satisfied that the darkest hour
is just before day) we stumbled on Fitzgerald's planta-

GENERAL A. B. McCALMONT,
April, 1865.

tion, and I made the house brigade headquarters. It is a large and comfortable building, well supplied with feather beds. The furniture is good. Some of our musicians played the piano this evening. A chaplain went out to invite Fitzgerald's daughters to play for us. They declined. The chaplain seemed to think their conduct very unreasonable. I told him, what is the fact, that the girls have three brothers in Lee's army, and referred him to a similar incident in an old history, where some people hung their harps on the willows and sat down and wept.

Our business now is guarding the South Side railroad, and the trains on the main pike running along it. We are relieved at each point by troops from the rear as fast as the movements of the army render an advance on our part necessary, and they seem to be going pretty fast. I think the most ardent avocate of a forward movement of the Army of the Potomac would have grumbled a little if he had been in my shoes last night. A battle had been going on all day in front. The sound of the cannon had shown steady progress westward till sundown. We had all retired at 9 o'clock, when an order came to move out immediately. We accordingly put in the night coming from Wilson's station to this point. Every day had been about the same, but it is easier than fighting, and even fighting now is not what it used to be. The enemy is beaten.

The news to-day is very cheering. Many prisoners were captured yesterday and 17 cannon; more prisoners are reported to-day. Ord was in Burkesville before Lee reached it. Lee is compelled to re-cross the Appomattox. The number of prisoners reported to-day is about 13,000. From the sound of the cannon I judge that there has been no determined stand made by the enemy. Lee will not be able to unite with Johnston. Grant has out-generaled him. It looks as if the matter was about over, the dog dead and the child's name Anthony. The people here, though Southern in feeling, are tired of the war and broken in spirits. They will be glad when the end is announced, and the government restored. There may be more fighting, but I think not much. I trust the goal has been reached.

You will get earlier and more reliable news in the papers than I can furnish, but you will be glad to know that I am still safe and well. I have many more comforts than when I commanded a regiment, but there is not much danger that I will fall in love with war. It is a sad thing to follow in the rear of a defeated army, and yet it is the height of military success, and is very inspiring. Even at midnight our bands play while marching, and the men often cheer.

But I am beginning to feel chilly and will retire. The staff is snoring, part of it in the parlor, part of it upstairs in feather beds. I shall retire to that luxury, too. Hartranft's headquarters are in the woods to-night, about a quarter or half a mile farther up the road.

Nottaway C. H., Virginia,
April 9, 1865.

My Dear Brother:

This is a beautiful Sunday morning, in a very beautiful country. Our corps was assigned the duty of guarding the South Side railroad and wagon trains on the move from Petersburg. We have been working our way to keep up with the rapid progress of the army, and to protect the railroad, which is being rapidly placed in running order.

On Thursday night I made brigade headquarters at the house of a man named Fitzgerald. We had a very pleasant time of it, sleeping two nights in feather beds, but the weather has been so pleasant that I have cared very little either for houses or tents. Fitzgerald is a Methodist. He has three sons in Lee's army. Before I left him he desired to take the oath. Yesterday afternoon we moved on to this point, about three miles. At the edge of the village we met a vast drove of Rebel prisoners marching under guard in no kind of order. The road where we met them passes under an arch over which runs the railroad. We had to halt and wait till they all got through. They detained us nearly an hour, though they moved rapidly and were well closed up. Our bands (I have two in the brigade) played "Yankee Doodle," "Johnny Comes Marching Home," and other lively airs, while the procession passed. There were eight thousand three hundred prisoners in it. To see them coming through the opening at a double quick almost literally reached the idea of subjugation. The Romans passed their prisoners under an arch made of spears, called a yoke (sub jugum). I think the railroad arch is an improvement on the arch of spears, and better embodies the elements of our success, while it is more suggestive of the results. The scene would do for a painter. There were a great many of our troops looking at the prisoners, and though there was some joking, I believe there was not an insulting word spoken.

The last stand made by Lee's reduced army was near Amelia Court House on Thursday. For some hours the cannonading was very spirited and it was kept up during the day. The result of the fight, as reported by Sheridan, was the capture of 13,000 prisoners, about 17 cannon, and some five or six Rebel Generals. In addition to this the troops commanded by Ord occupied the road beyond Burkesville. Lee's retreat toward Danville was cut off. There was a little distant firing yesterday, and I presume Lee has re-crossed the Appomattox and is trying to get to Lynchburg. Even in this attempt he will have some difficulty, but I do not see how he can make a successful stand any place. This army is very strong and very confident. I have no doubt the war is virtually ended.

General Hartranft wrote a letter to Stanton, recommending my brevet. I forwarded it. I presume I will be all right. Colonel —— does not stand very high, either for spirit or ability. He is at home on a twenty-day leave, wounded. Some very good men say a shell knocked some dust in his eye. That was what they told me when I asked if he was wounded seriously. The Adjutant, who is his friend, says he thinks —— will not return at the expiration of his leave, and that his eye is pretty seriously injured.

Our corps headquarters were here last night, but have moved to Burkesville. The weather is lovely. The trees are coming into leaf. Fruit trees are in bloom. At night

the frogs and whipporwills make a merry chorus. Nature
seems to be rejoicing. The wheat fields on our way give
promise of subsistence not to armies, but to an humbled
and repentent people.

While at Fitzgerald's I read in the Bible some. There
was one touching passage in the close of the book of
Kings about the rebuilding of the temple. I marked a
verse where the old men who had seen the first temple
wept aloud when the foundation of the new one was laid.
There will be many in this miserable southern country
who will witness the laying of the new foundation, and
who saw the old building in its grandeur. The restoration of the good and great things of antiquity is always
a sublime event. The country may well be glad.

And yet how many did not live to see it. Noble, brave
and self-sacrificing, they fell in the hour of gloom. Like
Moses, they did not reach the land to which they guided
others. Unlike him, they did not even rise to the summit which overlooked it, but fell unnoticed and unknown
in the barren way. It seems hard this bright morning,
when I think of some whom we knew; Hays, for instance, and Reno. I cannot help attempting to quote,
though I cannot do it accurately, Byron's tribute to How-
ard, who fell at Waterloo:

> "There have been tears and breaking hearts for thee,
> And mine were nothing had I such to give,
> But when I stood beneath the fresh free tree,
> Which living grows when thou didst cease to live,
> And saw around me the wide field revive
> With the fruits and fertile promise, and the Spring
> Come forth her work of gladness to contrive,
> With all her reckless birds upon the wing,
> I turned from all she brought to thou she could not bring."

Nottaway C. H., Virginia,
April 12, 1865.

My Dear Brother:

Since Lee's surrender we have been lying here going through all the old routine of military duty as if nothing unusual had happened. We furnish a great many safeguards to families in the neighborhood, and our pickets guard the railroad with as much vigilance as if an attack were every moment expected.

A train of cars passed us yesterday. It had General Grant and staff on it, so it was reported, and some said that General Lee was also on it.

Some people here desire to sell lands. Fine plantations can be bought for ten dollars an acre. One man offered me two hundred and fifty acres of beautiful improved land at that price. Another wishes to sell one thousand acres, with improvements, at twenty dollars. Considering the improvements, the proximity to the railroad and the admirable quality of the land, the price is very cheap. The climate here is delightful. Spring is earlier than with us, and the winters are very mild. The forest trees are all coming into leaf. Fruit trees are all in bloom. I presume there is an abundance of peaches. Tobacco is raised in great quantities, some farms have four, five and six tobacco houses on them.. A man could do worse than to come here and live. The stock of the South Side railroad could be bought cheap. It runs from Lynchburg to Petersburg. Any quantity of fine pine land on the Nottaway could be had for a low price.

The country is beautiful. The soil must be excellent. It produces wheat, corn, and tobacco in great quantities. It is perfectly free from stones. I believe money could be invested here now to great advantage.

I have not thought much about oil for some days. I am so glad that the war is over that I care very little about anything else. I presume we will soon go home.

General Hartranft wrote a letter to Secretary Stanton which will probably secure my brevet, but just now I should rather go home and attend to business than have any military promotion.

Nottaway C. H., Virginia,
April 13, 1865.

My Dear Brother:

Part of Sheridan's Cavalry returned to this point to-day. Sheridan's headquarters are in the village. For the Virginia spelling of the name, I refer you to the enclosed official paper.

I think we will be mustered out soon, but our division being composed of new troops, and not much reduced in numbers, may be retained till the last. I am anxious to go home and get at business. I can see many advantages in this country over ours in climate and soil, but I think the reasons in favor of resuming business in Franklin are imperative, and I shall go there as soon as possible. I would cheerfully waive the chances of a brevet to go soon, but the War Department has not the time to consider resignations, and the best I can do will be to wait patiently for a regular muster out along with my command. We have very pretty camps near the railroad on the edge of the village. It would be a pleasant trip for you to visit us.

Nottaway C. H., Virginia,
April 19, 1865.

My Dear Brother:

I have not received any letter from you nor any news from Franklin since I returned. It is now nearly a month since I left you. I presume you have written, but the mails have been at fault. The railroad to this point is in very poor order. The weather is, however, becoming more settled, and as the ground dries up the trains run with more regularity.

To-day we are observing the occasion of the President's funeral. No work has been done. Minute guns were fired at noon at Burkesville, about twelve miles off

I am still commanding the First Brigade, Colonel Diven not having returned. But this life is rather monotonous. I should like to be at home.

The weather is very warm. The Q. M. Department of our corps have orders to fit up their transportation for another campaign. I do not known what it means, but I do not apprehend there will be much more fighting. We have only about four months, at any rate.

I presume my promised promotion has been forgotten in the exciting scenes at Washington, but it will not cause me a single sigh. It is a very empty kind of honor, without pay. The only advantage is that one has rather better accommodations on a march while commanding a brigade, and if Diven returns I will have to go back to my regiment unless I am breveted.

Even the advantage of better quarters is a small one in fine weather and while lying still. So I cannot see that the promotion matter will affect me in any way worth mentioning.

Camp near Alexandria, Va.,
April 29, 1865.

My Dear Brother:

The surrender of Johnston announced this morning virtually closes the war. I have no idea that this corps will be sent South again. It will probably remain here until mustered out.

Yesterday I called at the hospital on Seventh street and saw some of our wounded officers. Captain Dalien, the little Frenchman, whom I mentioned with the funny recruiting experience, is lying with a bullet hole through his lungs. I am afraid he will not live. Near him lay a Lieutenant dying. He had been doing well, but secondary hemorrhage came on, and his eyes were fixed. His poor wife was sobbing as if her heart would break.

We are encamped in a beautiful spot two miles from town, near Fairfax Seminary, on the road leading to the seminary from King street.

Headquarters 1st Brig., 3rd Div., 9 A. C.,
May 2, 1865.

My Dear Brother:

We are still lying near the Fairfax Seminary. My headquarters are a few rods south of it on the road out from King street. We will probably remain here until "ze close of ze war." I think we will be mustered out before a month. The three month's extra pay provision, I am told, did not pass Congress. I have not examined the laws.

Our camps here present at sunset an animated scene, but you saw more troops here once when things were not so bright.

My promotion seems to have been lost in the big events of the month, and I am not very sorry. Its only real advantage would be the command of a brigade, and that I have now without it. It would be attended with the pecuniary inconvenience of buying a suit of clothes and equipments for about two hundred and fifty dollars, which I should never wear. I am fully reconciled of being overlooked.

Camp near Alexandria, Va.,
May 9, 1865.

My Dear Brother:

I went to Washington this morning about 10 o'clock. I have received your letter of the 5th this evening since returning. It was a rainy, cold, raw day, but I had a spring wagon with me (an incident new to a brigade commander) and was able to attend to business without much inconvenience. I called at Costello's. His wife, Catherine, used to live with us. They are in very good circumstances. Stopping at a bank to get a draft on Philadelphia to send to my wife, I observed two ladies in black depositing a large quantity of small notes. I inferred that it was the proceeds of some subscription. As they went out I recognized one as Mrs. Douglas, widow of Stephen A. At another place where I stopped to buy a keg of ale a very seedy looking individual passed along the pavement. He looked a little like Dr. Espy in his declining years, was evidently quite drunk. It was Robert I. Walker, the old Secretary of the Treasury under Polk. He has been going down hill for several years.

Dining at Hammock's eating house I met an officer from this brigade, who has been on special duty at the arsenal lately. He has been in charge of nine or ten persons who are implicated in the assassination plot. His account of his duties, of the treatment of the prisoners and of their behavior made me shudder. The prisoners were confined in separate cells, and each had a hood or mask fastened over his or her head and face. They saw no one. No one could see their features. The masks were not removed even to eat. This morning the whole party were taken to court-martial, and were still hooded. They were there placed near and facing each other. The masks were all suddenly removed. It was rather a novel fancy. There is something in the idea of such a meeting calculated to curdle a man's blood.

The trial of these persons before a court-martial is a very bold stretch of power. I cannot see that it is either necessary or wise. I should have given trial by jury its true position. As long as we have a Constitution it is worth sticking to. As for the criminals I should care very little whether they were hanged, strangled or drowned, and I should not have regarded it as a very great calamity if they had been lynched by the mob. But surely it is a great stretch of power and of constitutional law to try these people by a military commission. Perhaps there may be features in their case that bring them legitimately within military jurisdiction, but I am afraid it is otherwise, and that their trial, conviction and execution will only produce one of those fearful reactions so common in history, when the extreme measures of a powerful and successful administration suddenly change the sentiments of men to horror, disgust and solicitude for their own safety.

It is said that our division will not be mustered out as

9

soon as the rest of the Pennsylvania troops. Several orders and the location of our camps look that way. General Hartranft himself is put on duty in Washington, which will probably last all summer. A few days ago we were placed in a new camp out here on the Mt. Vernon road, two miles from Alexandria. An officer on Grant's staff intimated to me that we might be sent to Kentucky, but I think it is not probable. Still I believe we will be retained in service a month or more.

I have been troubled for a month past with rheumatism or lumbago. Lying in a tent this damp weather does not improve my symptoms. I think I shall wait a few weeks, and if we are going to be retained for provost duty during the summer, I shall resign. I would never make a good police officer. I have beside, some aversion to playing soldier in peace times. I should like to spend part of the summer at my leisure in some quiet place with my family, and not be troubled with anything.

Camp on Mt. Vernon Road,
May 12, 1865.

Dear Brother:

It is too cold to write this morning. Yesterday was warm and pleasant, but there was a severe thunderstorm in the evening. It kept up raining and blowing with almost incessant thunder and lightning half the night. This morning it is so cold that I can hardly hold a pen. I presume it will be very warm before two days.

The troops of the Second and Fifth Corps are beginning to arrive. The army of Sherman will not be far behind. The review will come off about the middle of next week.

Camp on Mt. Vernon Road,
May 25, 1865.

My Dear Brother:

I did not receive your letter, the one written at the Continental, until yesterday afternoon after returning from the review. It was then too late for a letter to reach you at New York, and beside, I was very tired.

This is a beautiful evening. The view from my tent is very fine. Between us and Alexandria twenty regiments are holding dress parade. The air is swimming with music. Far off stands the old capitol still untouched, and in all its beauty. Cheers and merry voices come up with the sounds of bands and drums. It all breathes peace and hope. Thank God, there is rest for the weary, even here.

The review was very grand. You ought to have spared the time and fatigue to witness it, but you could not have seen it all. It was too large for that. I looked at it till I was tired, and I presume I did not see the half of it.

We went across the river on Monday. Our division was placed away out east of the Capitol during Monday night. I established brigade headquarter at a lager beer garden. We had our own music, plenty of lager and a pretty good time generally.

The weather had been very bad previously, but Tuesday morning was perfectly clear. The sky wore a sort of Sunday look, and the air was just cool enough. We were ready at the hour appointed, and there was no delay in the movement. Everything went as if by clock work. The Ninth Corps started about 11 o'clock. Before we arrived at the Capitol a few friends made me dismount a moment to renew the assurance of their high consideration.

The sight of the Capitol was very imposing. Thousands of clean, well-dressed children were around it. They all had bouquets, and the whole scene was like a beautiful picture, but they clapped their little hands and cheered, and the mass of beauty moved like the flowers of the prairie in a summer breeze. The avenue was lined with people. House tops were covered and all windows filled. I thought the view of the people was better than that of the troops. It is a long distance from the Capitol to the President's when measured by the steady step. I think it is about a mile. To look back from the Treasury Building down the entire avenue, which filled with bayonets, glittered and moved like a river, was one of the most imposing sights I ever witnessed. And yet at almost any time during the two days you could see in it the same stream, but the waters were changing and moving on.

At Willard's some lively young fellows were doing the procession systematically on whisky and water. They had a large room with big windows in the front of the house. One of them, Colonel Shaffner, has been noted in ocean telegraph enterprises. He is now experimenting on the most effective mode of exploding powder and other combustibles. He and his friends gave me a welcome that was very amusing. They had loaded a lot of cartridges in a string. Shaffner, by his battery, exploded them all at once. It made quite a report. Then the party waved some sheets and pillow cases out of the window, and proposed three cheers for Colonel McCalmont. Some people below helped them a little. The thing took me by surprise, but I soon saw the joke and laughed as much as anybody. After the corps had passed I paid the room a visit, and had a fine view of the procession during the afternoon. The fellows were still keeping up their welcome. They had a printed program of the order of march, and they could thus recognize each regimental commander as he came along. Then they would call out his name, give him three cheers, and go through their usual salute. About 3 o'clock they seemed pretty tired, however, and the leader in the business, a wag from New York, announced to the satisfaction of all concerned that there were only six inches more of the thing to do. It occupied about a quarter of an hour longer.

A pleasant little circumstance to me personally occurred near the President's stand. I had ridden up there to look at the Fifth Corps, which made a fine appearance. After a time my old regiment, the One Hundred and Forty-second, passed. They gave three cheers for the President, and just afterward three more for the "old commander," as Geary has it. I can assure you I felt the compliment, and felt for my handkerchief at the same time.

I stayed in town Tuesday night, and saw the review on Wednesday. There is not much difference in the appearance of the two armies. Two or three divisions of Sherman's army spoiled their display by marching without their bayonets fixed.

The whole thing was very grand. I looked at it by the hour until I was tired. You could do that, and go away without any danger of missing the show. You could sleep, if you were so disposed, and on waking up the same eternal glittering river of bayonets was still flowing on. There was some variety in it, too; half a dozen regiments of Zouaves, with their fancy dresses, gave quite a gay appearance to the Fifth Corps. Some of the bands were magnificent. Occasionally the consolidated martial music of a brigade, thirty or fifty drums all beating some lively air, would make one's heart throb, though I had begun to think a drum corps rather a dilapidated institution.

We are working to get mustered out. I think our division will go to Harrisburg early next week, perhaps Monday. I am kept very busy; am president of a court-martial, with more cases to try than will ever be heard. Also recorder of a board to pass on merits of all commissioned officers of the division. I will have to work all the time. Colonel Diven has been discharged. I care nothing now for a brevet. It will be of no value. I am entirely satisfied with everything. I shall leave with no unkind feelings toward any person. I hope soon to see you all at home.

Harrisburg, Pa., June 2, 1865.

My Dear Brother:

I came here with the regiment this morning about sunrise. We saw very few people on the street. My wife and the children were, however, dressed and, of course, glad to see me. I did not go out to camp with the regiment, but remained in town and took breakfast. Afterward I went to camp, and was annoyed somewhat by the pompous airs of a little captain, who is in charge of the premises, and who is drawing all the water in the small channel of his authority. Our men are well quartered. They will be paid in a few days, and then we will be done with the thing. We are already mustered out.

We are all in good health. I received an appointment as Brevet Brigadier General, but the notice did not reach me until an hour after we were actually mustered out of the service. I suppose under the circumstances it would be hardly proper to accept it, but the compliment is all there is in it, and that is just as strong as it would be with a formal acceptance.

Metalmark Books is a joint imprint of The Pennsylvania State University
Press and the Office of Digital Scholarly Publishing at The Pennsylvania State
University Libraries. The facsimile editions published under this
imprint are reproductions of out-of-print, public domain works that hold
a significant place in Pennsylvania's rich literary and cultural past.
Metalmark editions are primarily reproduced from the University Libraries'
extensive Pennsylvania collections and in cooperation with other
state libraries. These volumes are available to the public for viewing online
and can be ordered as print-on-demand paperbacks.

LIBRARY OF CONGRESS CATALOGING-IN-PUBLICATION DATA

McCalmont, Alfred B., 1825–1874.
[Extracts from letters from the front during the
War of the Rebellion]
Extracts from letters written by Alfred B. McCalmont,
1862–1865 / Alfred B. McCalmont.
p.   cm.
Originally published under title: Extracts from letters
from the front during the War of the Rebellion.
Franklin, Pa. : R. McCalmont, 1908.
"Metalmark Books."
Summary: "A selection of letters written by Alfred B. McCalmont
to family members from the American Civil War front from September
1862 to June 1865, covering his service as a colonel in the 142nd and 208th
Pennsylvania infantry. First published in 1908 for private
circulation"—Provided by publisher.
ISBN 978-0-271-05385-1 (pbk. : alk. paper)
1. McCalmont, Alfred B., 1825–1874—Correspondence.
2. United States—History—Civil War, 1861–1865—
Personal narratives.
3. United States. Army. Pennsylvania Infantry Regiment,
142nd (1862–1865).
4. United States. Army. Pennsylvania Infantry Regiment,
208th (1864–1865).
5. Soldiers—Pennsylvania—Venango County—Correspondence.
6. Venango County (Pa.)—Biography.
I. Title.

E601.M13 2012
973.7'448—dc23
2011046810

Printed in the United States of America
Reprinted by The Pennsylvania State University Press, 2012
University Park, PA 16802-1003

The University Libraries at Penn State and the Penn State University Press,
through the Office of Digital Scholarly Publishing, produced this volume to
preserve the informational content of the original. In compliance with current
copyright law, this reprint edition uses digital technology and is printed on
paper that complies with the permanent Paper Standard issued by the
National Information Standards Organization (ANSI Z39.48–1992).